HOW TO USE
A CONSULTANT
IN YOUR COMPANY

HOW TO USE
A CONSULTANT
IN YOUR COMPANY
A Managers' and
Executives' Guide

John J. McGonagle and Carolyn M. Vella

John Wiley & Sons, Inc.
New York • Chichester • Weinheim • Brisbane • Singapore • Toronto

Published by John Wiley & Sons, Inc.

Published simultaneously in Canada.

This publication is designed to provide accurate and authoritative information in regard to the subject matter covered. It is sold with the understanding that the publisher is not engaged in rendering professional services. If professional advice or other expert assistance is required, the services of a competent professional person should be sought.

Library of Congress Cataloging-in-Publication Data:

McGonagle, John J.
    How to use a consultant in your company: a managers' and executives' guide/John J. McGonagle and Carolyn M. Vella.
      p. cm.
    Includes index.
    ISBN 0-471-38727-4 (alk. paper)
    1. Business consultants—Selection and appointment. I. Vella, Carolyn M.
II. Title.
HD69.C6 M388 2001
658.4'6—dc21
                                        00-063339

Printed in the United States of America.

10 9 8 7 6 5 4 3 2 1

CONTENTS

Contents

Contents

Contents

Contents

Contents

1

INTRODUCTION

"In 1997, operations and IT masters Andersen Consulting [now Accenture] and Deloitte Consulting showed, respectively, 21 percent and 30 percent growth in revenues, while strategy shops McKinsey and the Boston Consulting Group reported growth of 10 and nine percent in that year."[1]

Today we are in what is being called a "golden age of consulting."[2] And while there are two sides to every consulting relationship, it seems that the consultant side of the equation has most, if not all, of the tools needed to create and control that relationship.

For those seeking to enter the consulting business or to grow a consulting practice, the literature is vast and growing rapidly:

- A quick search at a site such as Amazon.com produces more than one hundred titles in print for the consultant (or would-be consultant).

- The magazine literature on opportunities in consulting continues to grow as the hiring by consultant firms continues to grow.[3]
- Consultants have publications of their own, including *Consultants News, Consulting,* and *What's Working in Consulting.*
- Consultants are using the Internet for assistance in developing and conducting their practices. For example, more and more web sites are aimed at helping consultants in their practice, helping them land assignments, and helping them do their business better. They include:

Guru.com (http://www.guru.com/).

Onvia Business Services
(http://www.onvia.com/usa/services/).

Starbelly.com (http://www.starbelly.com/).

The Vault (http://www.vault.com).

On the other hand, the businesses (the consultants' clients) seeking to hire and effectively use consultants have very little such help. In fact, they often face a double challenge: finding the right consultants *and* getting the most out of them.[4]

We have written this book for both the manager and the executive who customarily use consultants or may be thinking of hiring one.

In our experience, which encompasses both sides of the consulting relationship, the success of every consulting relationship depends on the extent and depth of the mutual understanding and agreement between the consultant and his or her client. That understanding must eventually be incorporated into a written agreement that serves as the statement of retention as well as a management guide for both parties.

Because the relationship is contained in a document—the consulting agreement or contract—many on both sides of the client-consultant relationship believe that they need to pay little attention to the contractual issues. They assume that once the parties agree that the retention is to begin, the rest of the process involves standard terms and conditions.

One of the first concepts both clients and consultants must accept is that there is no such thing as a standard consulting relationship, and therefore there is no standard consulting agreement. That is not only because each project is unique, but also because the relationship between the consultant and client is highly malleable; it can be worked into virtually any form the parties may choose.

Unfortunately, if the two sides are not careful, that relationship can evolve or devolve into a form that neither has chosen but that both sides are still responsible for having created. So when business executives and managers are presented with a situation of such variety and complexity, it is very useful to have help, suggestions, and guidelines.

To satisfy that need, *How to Use a Consultant in Your Company: A Managers' and Executives' Guide* is several books in one:

- It defines consulting, the client-consultant relationship, and the duties of the parties. It explains the roles that corporate policies, contracts, and agreements play in directing the consultant's work. In addition, it focuses on and clarifies the duties and obligations of corporate personnel at each executive and management level with respect to the consulting relationship.
- It deals with how to manage that relationship, once it has been created, by giving the business executive and manager clear, experienced guidance. We hope this will compensate for all the advice available to consultants!
- *How to Use a Consultant in Your Company: A Managers' and Executives' Guide* has a considerable how-to-do-it aspect. Because the contract between client and consultant ought to be a key element in creating, defining, and controlling the client-consultant

relationship, we have included language and forms that can be used by the manager or executive as models. We explain how to adapt these clauses and forms to fit your own situation, and we show the advantages (and in some cases, disadvantages) of each alternate clause or paragraph. Other materials provide help in developing formal company policies on hiring consultants, billing procedures, and ways of evaluating the consultant's work.

Nonprofits and government bodies have operational concerns and problems different from those of private businesses. But when they are consumers of consulting services, they face many of the same issues as do their private sector counterparts. Thus, while we do not specifically mention it in the text, the principles and even some of the contract language presented in this book are often appropriate for use by such organizations.

USER NOTES

Throughout the book, we have used a variety of forms, contract language samples, extracts from policy documents, and so on.[5] The contract language and company policy samples are set in their own distinctive typefaces so that you can easily find them in the text.

For ease of discussion, the institution hiring a consultant will generally be called the *client,* by which we mean a business, although individuals and governments also hire consultants. The term *consultant* will be used whether the consultant is a partnership, an individual, a corporation, or even a university.

Where we can, we quote real clients and real consultants to emphasize our point. These remarks are usually boxed and are put into a newspaper-style font so that you know we are quoting a real, identifiable source.

In a few instances, we found it necessary to use an actual or fictitious example to illustrate a point. If the former, we direct you to where you can read more about that very case; if the latter, we clearly indicate that it is a fictitious case. In some examples, we found that the hints we have for you or the issues you will face may vary due to the identity of the consulting firm. For that reason, we have created two entirely fictional consulting firms for use in our examples:

- The first, CMV & Associates, is a small firm, with fewer than five full-time consultants. Like many such firms, it is newer, and run by its founder(s).
- The second, McGonagle & Company, is a multicity, international, long-established firm. It is being run by partners/owners who are one or more generations removed from the founder(s).

The book is designed to be read and to be used. By that, we mean the manager should feel free to dip into it to look for help. Because the consulting relationship is a complex one, some concepts, such as the way in which the work being done by the consultant is described, are touched on in several places. We have tried to strike the proper balance between redirecting the manager and repeating our comments. The order in which information is presented in the book reflects the way the relationship should develop. Because the most effective relationships are ones where all key issues are handled at the beginning, the final consulting agreement will be affected by concepts and issues raised in every chapter.

NOTES

1. "Companies Fall out of Love with Consultants," 1999, http://www.vault.com (December 14, 1999).

2. Executive from consulting firm, IBM Global Services, quoted in Edward Wakin, "Getting the Most out of Consultants," *Beyond Computing*, June 1999, 54–55.

3. See Brian Palmer, "Is It Time to Join the Consultants?" *Fortune*, August 3, 1998, 251 et seq.

4. Fordham University communications professor, quoted in Wakin, "Getting the Most out of Consultants," 54.

5. Some of the suggested contract and policy language first appeared in John McGonagle's earlier book *Managing the Consultant: A Corporate Guide* (Radnor, PA: Chilton Books, 1980).

2

CONSULTING:
THE BIG PICTURE

WHAT IS CONSULTING?
THE MANAGEMENT CONTEXT

The diversity of the consulting industry, properly consulting industries, is remarkable. Consultants are found in virtually every field. There are:

- Consulting engineers, one of the oldest sectors of the consulting business.
- Accounting firms, which also provide management consulting services.
- Management consulting firms, which provide executive and employee recruitment and compensation services, in addition to their traditional role of the "identification, diagnosis, and resolution of business issues."[1]

- Advertising firms, which also offer separate media consulting services.
- Political consultants, advising individuals on how best to get elected.
- Consultants who provide advice only on specific corporate processes, such as competitive intelligence.
- Advisors to the top management of the giant corporations of the world on the very core of their businesses, strategies, structures, finances, marketing, and personnel operations.
- Specialists in the very narrowest of market niches, such as consulting firms specializing in providing advice about the restructuring, acquisition, merger, and dissolution of medical practices.

Where consultants appear and how often they appear is almost impossible to list. However, consulting may be the most diverse and most broadly based business today. Moreover, that reach increases, rather than shrinks, each day:

- Consultants advise the world's great corporations on the creation of new products and may assist in their actual development.
- In government, consultants are very often at the right hand of policymakers, providing studies and advice. Critics of the federal government's consulting procurement processes have asserted that very often the consultants themselves are the policymakers, serving without the control of the agency and not subject to congressional supervision or confirmation.
- Consultants provide direct services. They set up computer systems, even purchasing the components on behalf of their clients. They also serve individuals in the political process, steering potential candidates through the intricacies of complying with federal and state election laws.
- Consultants are a tremendous source of research, both primary and secondary, whether done under

contract for one client or for a group of clients. For this reason, it is not surprising that many consultants come from the academic community. In fact, many academics serve as part-time consultants in some capacity.

- Consulting firms often provide a process. There are consults providing studies and advice on marketing, cash flow management, data management, storage, transportation, telecommunications, and many other processes related to the final output of an institution. Very often these processes dominate the activities of the institution, so that by providing guidance the consulting firm may, to an extent not realized by all parties, be setting the ultimate direction of the institution.

Today, the consulting industry is huge. How large is it? According to one recent estimate, the current revenue of the "Big Five" consulting firms alone exceeds $43 billion,[2] and the overall size of the consulting industry may exceed $100 billion.[3] And the consulting industry is still growing— 20 percent per year by one estimate.[4] Why? One answer lies in the steps taken by many companies to become more competitive—steps, it should be noted, taken with the advice of consultants:

[In the 1980s, workforces] were cut, just-in-time inventories were added and extra controls were taken on to track productions.... Now lean operations may have come back to haunt [U.S. companies].[5]

Definitions

If we look to one dictionary's definition of *consult*, we find the following:

Etymology: Middle French or Latin; Middle French *con-sulter*, from Latin *consultare*, frequentative of *consulere* to deliberate, counsel, consult... *intransitive* senses

1 : to consult an individual ...
3 : to serve as a consultant[6]

And for *consultant*, we find this:

Function: *noun*

1 : one who consults another
2 : one who gives professional advice or services[7]

Interestingly, each of these terms is related to *consul*, a term applied to senior officials who carry official authority and power. Thus, the dictionary says that consulting is something that is done by consultants.

It is useful to review some of the many attempts others have made to define *consultant*. Many such attempts have been undertaken by the federal government. They arise from initiatives to limit the use of consultants, to control the role consultants play in policymaking, to keep consultants from managing the execution or implementation of government programs, or to keep consultants from being hired when they may pose a conflict of interest.

"'Consultant,' a universal term for any professional who provides assistance to others, usually for a fee."[8]

Each definition has reflected an attempt to define a consultant in a way that advances management or control objectives. Thus, one government agency may define a consultant broadly to allow it to hire consultants, while another agency may define a consultant quite narrowly, so that it is not prevented, by conflict-of-interest regulations, from hiring consultants for a needed project. Congress may define consultant in its very broadest and most generic sense to provide legislation governing the employment and use of consultants; the Office of Personnel Management may distinguish a consultant from a temporary employee for certain personnel purposes.

Consulting has been the subject of many humorous definitions as well. Here are three classics:

- One comes from *The Devil's Dictionary,* where Ambrose Bierce defines the verb *consult* as "to seek another's approval of a course already decided upon."
- A second defines a consultant as "someone who, when you ask the time, takes your watch, reads the time, tells you—and then keeps the watch."
- A third defines a consultant as "anyone with a brief-case who is at least 50 miles from home."

In consulting, as in so much of business, humor often conceals the cutting edge of truth. So what truths do these classic jibes contain?

- *To seek another's approval of a course already decided upon.* Consultants can all sadly confirm that they have been offered assignments with a hidden agenda. It may be that a decision, usually one with negative impacts such as layoffs, has already been made, or is inevitable. But management believes that the move can be made more palatable to those who will be affected. So, for some managers, it is easier to have an outsider deliver bad news than to do it themselves.

- *Someone who, when you ask the time, takes your watch, reads the time, tells you—and then keeps the watch.* Consultants bring to a retention an ability to cut through the clutter. They more often than not use the client's resources, perhaps even to the point of having an office on-site. They are resented because what they appear to do is give back to a client a solution that should have been obvious to the client. And then they charge—often dearly—for it.
- *Someone with a briefcase who is at least 50 miles from home.* One often finds some odd perceptions among the client community about who are the better consultants. One is that "there are no good consultants around here," wherever *here* is. This is as obviously false as the concept that it is often better to hire a big, well-known firm than a smaller, lesser-known one. And some of the giants are notorious for keeping their staff on the road at all times.

From a review of these definitions and similar definitions in the private sector, the only conclusion that emerges is that a consultant provides consulting services and consulting services are provided by a consultant. This definition is not as circular as it seems. Clearly, a consultant is different from an employee. *Over time, the term consultant has been transformed from meaning one who provides advice to a business enterprise to one who provides advice or other business support services that cannot easily be classified elsewhere.*

The Client's Point of View

From a management perspective, clients use consultants to provide outside assistance from time to time for a wide variety of reasons. Here are some of the more commonly cited ones:

- The client is facing a shortage of expertise among existing personnel, and the nature of the work being done does not warrant the hiring of full-time personnel, even on a temporary basis. In that context, many consulting firms offer a concentration of specialties that makes their use a relative bargain.
- There is an immediate, overall shortage of staff. This can be because of hiring restrictions in government or personnel and budgetary restrictions in the private sector. Contracts are let to consultants because the consultant can provide management as well as staff not available at the time to the client hiring the consultant.
- There is a shortage of time. This often is combined with one of the above scenarios. That is, a given task or project must be performed quickly and the client's staff charged with completing the project is unable to meet the demands placed on it without outside, expert assistance.
- The client sees the need for an "objective," "independent," or "outside" point of view. Businesses and government agencies often are so enmeshed in their own problems or so limited in their institutional perspectives that they see, or at least think they see, the need to bring in fresh ideas to provide insight, guidance, or a solution to a current problem. And that means using outside expertise.
- The consultant possesses a unique set of skills or access to unique tools, methodologies, or technology. Here the retention is based on the fact that the client has already made an early determination about the scope of the problem and what it will take from the consultant to solve it.
- The consultant provides a perspective that the client lacks. That may be due to experience with other

firms in the same or a similar industry; or it may be due to experience with similar problems and issues in very different industries.

- The consultant is expected to serve as a catalyst within the client organization to help generate changes, in addition to helping to identify those that are really needed.
- The consultant will work within the client organization to transfer state-of-the-art skills and information. This may be through having client personnel work with the consultant, or the client may use the consultant to conduct formal seminars or one-on-one coaching.

The Consultant's Point of View

From the perspective of the consultant, consulting means a wide variety of things, some of which are conflicting:

- It is a way to use personal expertise only when and where the consultant wants.
- It means a perpetual process of selling, of looking toward the next retention.
- It means self-employment, with all of its attendant challenges, benefits, and pitfalls.
- It means working in a large organization, under pressure to perform.
- It is a way to exploit new areas of demand in the marketplace.
- It is a transitional stage between corporate jobs.
- It is a permanent commitment to "working for yourself."
- It is a way to describe a job that cannot be otherwise described accurately.

Some consultants are happy to be described as *consultants,* while others prefer any term except consultant.

Some consultants will tell you, and to a degree properly, that *consulting* should be used as a term to describe only those firms that provide management consulting, that is, advice to senior management. Other branches, they assert, should describe themselves as process consultants, consulting engineers, and so on—that is, they should add a descriptive term before or after the word.

Those practitioners who disavow the term *consulting* do so for one or more of several reasons:

- It is a term without specificity, a catchall. Look in the yellow pages, they will say. You'll see about two dozen varieties of physicians, but how many different types of consultants do you see listed under "business consultants"?
- The term is often used in a humorous or sarcastic manner. The national cartoon strip *Dilbert* is one wonderful example of using consultants, as well as managers and coworkers, to make humorous statements.
- Businesses, nonprofits, and government agencies under pressure to cut costs often immediately cut back on "consulting." This knee-jerk reaction is done on the basis that "consulting" is not a mission-critical expenditure. And that inference troubles many practitioners.
- For some companies, consultants are really just a temporary, more flexible workforce, operating under another name. They are retained as long as needed, and when the client no longer needs their specific services, there is no messy or expensive termination.

"The responsibility for curing bad consultant behavior lies just as much with the customers as it does with the consultants—a combination of the

(Continued)

15

(Continued)

old adage, 'Physician, heal thyself,' and that brand-new saying, 'Patient, give thyself a stiff dose of accountability.' After all, it's asking a lot of any company to selflessly and voluntarily curtail lucrative revenue streams, unethical or not. Don't forget that a consultancy exists to make money, just as any corporation does."[9]

THE LEGAL CONTEXT

It is not only consultants and their clients who help define consulting. The legal aspects of that relationship can be complex.

What Is Consulting?

Given the diverse approaches to consulting and that the consultant is really a creature of the modern business and industrial world, to understand what a consultant is, one needs to understand the legal nature of the consulting relationship.

A Legal Analysis

Basically, the status of consultant is conferred only by an agreement between two parties; there is no such thing as a consultant as a matter of law.

The consulting agreement, as used today, is often just a bastard child of the employment contract and the contract that has created the independent contractor relationship, such as in the construction field.

In the case of the employment contract, sometimes called a contract of service, traditionally the employer selects the employee, is responsible for payment of wages, establishes compensation, provides direction, controls the employee's method of doing work, manages the workplace, and supervises or dismisses the employee. With these managerial prerogatives come legal obligations arising out of a whole complex of legal notions encompassed under the phrase *employment relationship*. These obligations include the following:

- *Agency.* When an employer hires and supervises an employee, the employee is to act only in the employer's interests while on the job. Although subordinate to the employer, an employee may be the agent for the employer so that an employee can legally bind the employer.
- *Vicarious liability.* The damages an agent or employee inflicts on others are most often the responsibility of the employer. The employer, not the employee, must compensate the victim of the employee's mistakes.
- *Regulation of the workplace.* Employers are required to provide safe workplaces for employees and workers' compensation insurance to compensate injured workers for business-related accidents or illnesses.

Under the classic independent contractor relationship, on the other hand, an employer hires an expert or specialist to do a certain task but retains no supervision or daily control over how the expert accomplishes that task. This means, among other things, that the employer has no direct control over the specialist's own employees. In this way, the employer is protected from certain legal and managerial liabilities in exchange for surrendering certain managerial prerogatives. The reasons for entering into this relationship, which is the basis of the consulting relationship, are varied. Several are commonly advanced and are akin to the reasons usually given for hiring a consultant. The reasons most often given for hiring independent contractors are the following:

- A company has a limited or onetime need for specialized skills.
- The contractor has unique areas of expertise.
- Limitations on corporate wage scales keep a company from hiring employees to do the work in question.
- The specific skills needed are unavailable in the current labor market.
- A company needs rapid access to the latest technology and experience in its application, which it does not possess.
- A company uses a contractor to provide multiple exposure to alternative solutions to new problems.
- An independent contractor has credibility as an outsider.
- Limitations on executive time prevent the company from being able to do what is necessary. An outsider must both do the work and supervise it.

In most cases, the consulting agreement falls between the contract of service, or the employment relationship, and the contract for services, or the independent contractor relationship. It is significantly closer to the latter than to the former but often may have elements of each. For example, the business contracts to receive the services of an expert but does not surrender all managerial or supervisory powers. The consultant is placed in the status of an independent contractor with the business; however, the scope of the consultant's task may be subject to continuing redefinition or even modification by the business as the assignment proceeds.

CONTRACT HINTS

In light of the special nature of the consulting agree-
(Continued)

18

(Continued)

ment and consulting relationship, several key topics should always be considered in the creation of the consulting relationship and thus, ultimately, in the consulting agreement itself:

1. The nature and scope of the services to be performed.
2. A statement that the consultant has the status of an independent contractor, including in his/her/its handling of the final work product.
3. Details about the payment of compensation and costs.
4. The length of the relationship.
5. How, when, and by whom the relationship can be terminated.
6. How the work to be performed can be changed, and by whom.
7. Special requirements (covenants) to protect the business, such as the handling of confidential information.
8. How to handle any disputes.
9. What remedies are available to whom on default or failure to perform, and what remedies are not available.
10. How formal notice is to be given, how changes in the scope of the assignment are to be memorialized, and so on.

Because of the complexity of the elements of the consulting relationship and consulting agreement, the relationship never should be entered into orally. In fact, it may be virtually impossible to create and enforce an oral—that is, nonwritten—consulting agreement. The chief problem in enforcing such a relationship is a legal principle known as the statute of frauds. That provides, in broad terms, that an oral contract is void if, by its terms, it cannot be performed within one year after the contract is made.

Even if a contract is originally oral but survives the statute of frauds, the enforceability of a renewal may be affected by the statute. For example, the renewal of a written contract for a period of one year for a second year requires something in writing, even though each separate contract is within the applicable one-year statute of frauds.

Isn't Calling It a Consulting Contract Enough?

Many people believe that if the parties merely call an individual a consultant, he or she becomes a consultant. *Stating in a consulting agreement that the consultant is an independent contractor vis-à-vis the business does not automatically create the desired independent contractor relationship.* However, oddly enough, the failure to make this statement can be held against the parties. So a statement that the parties have this relationship is a good starting place.

But common experience should be enough to tell you that a label is not all you need. For example, radio advertisements for carpets or vacations often ask you to call "one of our consultants." But such people are not independent advisors: They are paid by the seller in the form of salary, commission, or both. They are not independent of the seller, but rather employees or sales agents. The term is used to make you think that their advice is neutral or independent.

In fact, it is their financial interest in completing the transaction that deprives them of the independence needed to be called consultants. Keep this concept in mind when considering how true consultants are to be compensated.

In preparing any agreement between a consultant and a client, the preparer should *never* call the client an employer. That simple mistake could later be used to undermine the contention of either or both parties that the consultant is, for the purposes of the agreement, an independent contractor.

20

By establishing that the relationship between the client and the consultant is that of an independent contractor, the business is giving up the right to direct and control the consultant and the consultant's employees, both in the outcome and in the manner and means by which that outcome is obtained. This is the essence of the independent contractor (consultant) relationship. The business must always respect this allocation of control. That is because in any challenge, such as by the Internal Revenue Service, a court will look beyond the language of the agreement to the actual conduct of the parties to determine their true relationship.

For example, if a court must decide whether the wrongs (torts) of a consultant are the responsibility of a client, which presumably has substantially greater assets to pursue, the court will not stop at a document. If the court determines, based on facts, that the client has been exercising control over the consultant or the consultant's employees, including over the manner and means in which the work assigned to the consultant is being conducted, the court may find that despite the language of the agreement, the relationship is that of employer to employee. This then would subject the business to what is known as "vicarious liability" for the torts of what would then be deemed "borrowed" employees, meaning that although the consultant and its employees working on the project are not on the payroll of the business, they are presumed to have been loaned to the business or borrowed by the business. In that case, the business can be sued successfully for any torts committed by the consultant and its employees.

Another critical element in determining what a consultant is lies in the ability of the client to control the nature of the task. That is, the client may wish to be able to modify the task from time to time without impinging upon the manner in which the task is accomplished. Both for reasons of the statute of frauds and because of the dangers of attributing the wrongs of a consultant's employees to the corporation, all modifications of the agreement and the relationship, including specific instructions and directions, must be in writing. If the parties are careful and make such directions in writing, they have provided protection from a legal standpoint as well as a management standpoint.

Thus, we have come full circle. A consultant provides consulting services, and consulting services are provided by a consultant. It is clear that a consultant is not an agent; nor is a consultant a partner or a joint venturer or an employee. A consultant is not merely an independent contractor but is closer to an independent contractor than to any of the other traditional legal forms. As the consultant is a nontraditional creature of the law, extreme care must be taken from both a legal and management point of view to ensure that the relationship is clearly established, maintained, and terminated.

The parties entering into a consulting relationship carry the risk that the relationship does not exist unless they carefully and clearly define it; they also enjoy the advantage that they can make the relationship what they want to make it when they want and for the purposes they want. From a legal point of view, ambiguities in that relationship can be either dangerous or beneficial. From a management point of view as well, the ambiguities present opportunities as well as perils.

If the parties work together to define the nature of the relationship and the need for the kinds of services sought, the relationship will work to their mutual benefit and satisfaction. If the parties are unable to answer the legal questions, they most likely will be unable to answer the management questions. Clear thinking in one area reflects clear thinking in the other.

How Does Consulting Differ from Other Business Relationships?

While consulting relationships sometimes look like other relationships, such as employment or contracting out, there are important distinctions.

Employee(s)

All clients must keep in mind one overriding consideration: By its actions, a client can "convert" a consultant from being an independent contractor into being an employee.

> "Once you say they [consultants or contractors] are your employees for some purposes, it's hard to maintain they're not for other [purposes]."[10]

That conversion carries with it severe consequences:

- Under federal income tax rules, "an employer does not generally have to withhold or pay any taxes on payments to independent contractors."[11] But, "you [the client] will be liable for social security and Medicare taxes and withheld income tax if you do not deduct and withhold them because you treat an employee as a nonemployee."[12] In other words, if the IRS determines, after the fact, that an independent contractor was really an employee, you are now the employer and must pay all federal taxes you should have withheld from payments to the independent contractor.
- If the person or persons whom you treated as consultants (or independent contractors) should be found to have been employees, you may also find that they are entitled, retroactively, to benefits you provided to your regular employees but not to them. While most companies might immediately think about medical insurance benefits, these individuals may also be, retroactively, eligible for profit sharing, employee investment plans, stock options, and other significant financial advantages. There are other nontax consequences of crossing this divide. For example, state law may allow employees access to their personnel files.[13]

How much of a problem is this? The problem may be very widespread. Up to half of the eight million independent contractors and consultants now working in the United States may be misclassified and, under IRS criteria, should be reclassified as employees.[14]

What then, from a legal standpoint, is the difference between an employee, on the one hand, and an independent contractor/consultant on the other?[15] Under U.S. common law, *anyone who performs services, full-time or part-time, for you is your employee if you can control what will be done and how it will be done.* This is true even when you give the employee freedom of action. What matters is that you, the company, have the *right* to control the details of how the services are performed, and not what you may actually do in practice. In addition, if you have an employer-employee relationship, it makes no difference how it is labeled or what it is called. It is the *substance* of the relationship and *not its label* that determines the worker's legal status.

The general rule, then, is that an individual is an independent contractor only if you, the person or institution paying that individual, have the *right to control or direct only the result of the work but not the means and methods of accomplishing the result.*

To determine whether an individual is an employee or an independent contractor, you have to look at the total relationship between the worker and the business. In doing that, you must consider both the degree of control and the degree of independence in that relationship. The kinds of facts that are looked at to provide evidence of the degree of control and independence fall into three broad categories:

- Behavioral control;
- Financial control; and
- The type of relationship the parties have.

Behavioral control   What kinds of facts show whether a business has a right to direct and control how the worker does the task for which the worker is hired? They include the type and degree of instructions that the business gives the worker as well as the training that the business gives the worker.

Remember that an employee is generally subject to the business's instructions about when, where, and how to work. All of the following are examples of types of instructions about how to do work:

- When and where to do the work.
- What tools or equipment to use.
- What workers to hire or to use to assist with the work.
- Where to purchase supplies and services.
- What work must be performed by a specified individual.
- What order or sequence to follow in doing the work.

The amount of instruction needed varies widely depending on the type of job. For example, in some situations, a business may lack the knowledge to instruct some highly specialized professionals on how to do a job. In other cases, the task being done may require little or no instruction from the business. The key consideration is whether the business has retained the right to control the details of a worker's performance or has given up that right.

The training the business gives the worker can also be a consideration:

- An employee may be trained to perform services in a particular manner; but
- Independent contractors ordinarily use their own methods to perform services.

Financial control What facts show whether the business has a right to control the business aspects of the worker's job? They include information on business expenses, a worker's investment, the extent to which the worker makes his or her services available to others, how the business pays the worker, and the extent to which the worker can make a profit or suffer a loss:

- Independent contractors are more likely to have unreimbursed business expenses than are employees. That does not mean that the existence of such expenses is conclusive. Employees may also incur unreimbursed expenses in connection with services they perform for an employer.
- An independent contractor often has a significant investment in the facilities and equipment he or she uses in performing services for someone else. However, a significant investment is not absolutely necessary to establish independent contractor status.
- An independent contractor is generally free to seek out business opportunities. An independent contractor often advertises, usually maintains a visible business location, and is generally available to work for others in the relevant market.
- An employee generally receives a predetermined regular wage or salary for some period of time, that is, per hour, per week, or per month. That usually indicates that a worker is an employee, even if the wage or salary is supplemented, such as by a commission. On the other hand, an independent contractor is often paid a flat, negotiated fee for the entire job. However, some independent contractors, such as lawyers, may be paid based on an hourly rate for their work.
- An independent contractor can make a profit or suffer a loss.

Type of relationship   What kinds of facts show the type of relationship between the two parties? They include these:

- How written agreements describe the relationship the parties intend to create.

- Whether the business provides the worker with employee-type benefits. These are benefits such as insurance, a pension plan, vacation pay, or sick days.
- The permanence of the relationship. For example, let's say you hire a worker with the expectation that the relationship will continue indefinitely, rather than for a specific project or a set period. This is generally considered evidence that your intent was to create an employer-employee relationship.
- How critical the services performed by the workers are to your company's regular business. If a worker provides services that are a key aspect of your regular business activity, it is more likely that you will have the right to direct and control his or her activities. This would, in turn, tend to indicate an employer-employee relationship. For example, if a law firm hires a new attorney, it is likely that the firm will present that attorney's work as its own. It would thus have the right to control or direct that work.

Contracting Out

Contracting out, or outsourcing as it is more commonly known, is a major business and a growing one. For example,

> In the [1998–1999 year] alone, NASA paid $13 billion to seven outsource providers. Seneca Foods is now producing Green Giant canned goods for Pillsbury. In fact, the Dun & Bradstreet Barometer of Global Outsourcing reported that [in 1998] outsourcing dollars had increased by $40 billion from the previous year.[16]

Is contracting out different from consulting? Outsourcing is, strictly speaking, the process of arranging for entire business functions or processes to be handled by another company, governed by a long-term contract.

While the process may be transparent to third parties, such as to customers, the firm providing the outsourced services or products typically retains control over the means and manner of performance. Its obligation to its client is to provide goods or services of some specified quality measured against agreed-on performance measures.

Thus, most outsourcing contracts fit the classic definition of an independent contractor relationship. And, again in a parallel to some consulting relationships, "the question isn't whether a client company needs a service, but whether the outsource provider has the expertise and dedication to exceed the company's in-house ability."[17]

Internal Consultants

What are internal consultants? They are people who work for their clients on a permanent basis. They are corporate employees. The title they have derives from the work that they do and *not* from their legal relationship to the company.

The creation of internal consultants has as its goal to reduce the use of and reliance on specific types of consultants most often needed in large, diversified enterprises. These include management consultants, human resources consultants, operations management consultants, and information technology (IT) consultants. Thus, while they are internal, they are still professional. Many began as outside consultants and may even "bid" for internal assignments.

Internal consultants may operate in several different roles, depending on the corporate culture and need:

- They may analyze strategic business information and then make recommendations for action or serve as a think tank. These roles are quite similar to the roles played by external independent consultants.

- On the other hand, some of these units also are more actively involved in ongoing corporate initiatives, such as motivating change, serving as an internal champion of new ideas, or providing a completely confidential source for critical data needed by senior management for highly sensitive decisions.[18]
- In some companies, internal consultants operate only in certain key areas of interest that cross unit lines, such as information technology.

In general, companies with internal consultants find that outside consultants are most often still needed and are most effective in the following common situations:

- The company cannot afford or does not need a full-time internal consultant for the particular area of concern.
- The company needs additional assistance for a short amount of time or in connection with projects for which the internal consultant does not have the time.
- The company's internal consultants, or other company employees, lack either the specific expertise needed for a particular situation or do not have the broad experience needed for that situation.
- Company politics demand objectivity, neutrality, or at least the appearance of objectivity or neutrality provided by a nonemployee.

CONSULTING IS BIG BUSINESS—
BECAUSE IT IS VITAL

So let's get a handle on it! First, we will establish some basic concepts about the consultant-client relationship. Then, we will move on to discussing what works, what does not, and how to create the relationship and manage it better.

"When do you bring in a consultant? The answer is simple. Hire a consultant when their fees cost less than doing the project yourself."[19]

A quick way to summarize all the issues involved in deciding to use a consultant may be to ask yourself whether using a consultant will cost you less than doing it (whatever it is) yourself. That cost can be measured in terms of available time, the costs and difficulties of hiring needed expertise, or the costs involved in learning to do the work yourself.[20]

Getting more specific, let's take a look at the client-consultant relationship.

Do You Need a Consultant?

"Hiring a consultant can make sense if you need to know something about yourself or your leadership skills that you can't find out on your own because no one will tell you.... [B]ut that's not a multi-year assignment.... [M]ake sure there's a very discrete, tangible reason you're bringing somebody in."[21]

The first step in determining whether you need a consultant is to define the problem you think you are facing. Defining the problem is not as simple as it may seem. Before you make the decision to hire a consultant, you should answer the following questions:

- What is the issue facing me?
- What do I think needs to be done? Is it a process or an ultimate goal?
- Are there ways to measure success? What are they?

- How quickly must the problem be resolved? What resources are available in terms of personnel and money?
- What, because of constraints such as financial capacity or regulations, cannot be done?
- What do we want as the end product of a consulting relationship?
- What do we need as the end product of a consulting relationship?
- What operations might be affected by an attempt to solve the perceived problem?
- Do I have a buy-in from at least the levels of management whose help will be required to complete the assignment or who will be using the results of the retention?
- How will the consultant access our information and personnel?

What Makes Up the Consulting Relationship?

It would seem obvious that the parties to the process would be the (potential) client and the consultant seeking the retention. However, that is not completely accurate.

The potential client should always keep in mind that the average consultant seeks to contact and deal with F-U-N clients as much as possible. What is that? A F-U-N client is one who

- Has the *funds* and the power to spend them;
- *Understands* what is involved in working with a consultant; and
- *Needs* the services that the consultant can provide.

> "[CEOs] know their own limitations . . . so they think they need consultants
> *(Continued)*

(Continued)

to compensate for their failings. Consultants typically are overdeveloped in one particular skill, . . . and that can make them seem particularly useful to a CEO who isn't a superstar at anything."[22]

As for a consultant, he or she should keep in mind that a client tends to look for one who is a J-O-Y to work with. What is that? A J-O-Y consultant is one who

- Has done this type of *job* before and will be doing this one personally;
- Can *obligate* his firm to the retention being discussed; and
- Listens to *you* when you describe your problem and needs.

The authors of *Dangerous Company: Management Consultants and the Businesses They Save and Ruin* assert that the horror stories they relate raise these key issues for any potential client to resolve before beginning any management consultant retention:

1. Why are you doing this? . . .
2. That being achieved, ask yourself, do I need outsiders to help reach this goal? . . .
3. If I hire a consulting company, which characters will they send? . . .
4. What will it cost? (And how long will it take?). . . .
5. Never give up control. . . .
6. Don't be unhappy for even a day. . . .
7. Beware of glib talkers with books. . . .
8. Value your employees. . . .
9. Measure the process. . . .
10. If it's not broke, don't try to fix it.[23]

Our Top 10 List

We have organized the balance of this book in the form of a dialogue. At the beginning of each chapter, we present one or more of the top 10 things we see that cause the failure of consulting relationships (see the accompanying box).

**TOP 10 WAYS TO MAKE SURE
YOU DO NOT GET VALUE FROM
YOUR CONSULTING RELATIONSHIPS
(THE MORE YOU DO, THE LESS VALUE
YOU CAN BE SURE YOU WILL GET)**

1. Don't ever have the final decision maker or end user involved in interviewing potential firms. (Alternate: Always make sure the decision about whom to hire and what they are doing is made for someone else and on their, not your, budget.)
2. Let the consultant define the task or tasks and make sure that they get done.
3. Allow someone to retain a firm for which he or she previously worked.
4. Always select bigger over better. (Alternate: Pick a name other people know over one they do not.)
5. Don't ever talk about time or money.
6. Let the consultant put someone on the project you never met with.
7. Get it started with a handshake. You can always do the paperwork later.
8. Don't worry about supervision and reporting. Remember, they are the experts and you are merely the client.
9. Discuss the next stage of work (or better yet, another retention) well before this one is done.
10. Don't worry about defining what are to be the deliverables or how to measure them.

These 10 points seem humorous, but you should take them very seriously. In the chapters that follow, we will tell you more about these issues, why they are symptoms of major problems, and how to avoid them.

Help with Company Policy Statements

The use of formal, written company policies seems once again on the rise. However, the application of such policies to consulting relationships has always been problematic. In some companies, they are used as an indirect barrier to the use of *any* outside services. In other companies, they are written so awkwardly that they provide little real guidance.

Where we see that we can contribute to the development of sane and sensible company policy statements, we provide that help.

Help with Developing Contracts

Throughout the balance of this book, we have provided sample contract language. Our goal is to give the company that is party to the consulting relationship the tools to help build a contract that reflects its needs and the substance of the consulting relationship. However, and we cannot stress this point too much, *contracts should reflect the relationship agreed on.* The parties should not merely exchange documents and hope that they have created a sound relationship.

In using the contract language provided in this book, the client should always be aware that drafting a consulting agreement based on sample language has two advantages:

1. It forces both parties to think through and cover every area of importance to them; and

2. It provides sample, tested language that may be used to start to handle those points. If the sample language does not cover the points in the manner to which the parties have agreed, they can modify the language very simply.

The most effective way to use any form contract language is as a checklist. The clauses presented in this book are straightforward. They reflect attempts to create a working relationship between a consultant and a client. This in turn means trying to deal with potential problems obvious to both parties at the beginning of the contract, as well as with those problems that experience has shown can arise during the retention or in the event of a falling out between the parties.

Although contract language should not be added to agreements as mere protective armor, the decision to include a clause to deal with a portion of the relationship has merit. By doing so, the two parties are trying to cover even those circumstances they do not believe are likely to occur.

ILLUSTRATION—DRAFTING A COMPENSATION CLAUSE

A consultant's compensation can be as varied as the project on which the consultant is working. Agreements can provide for daily or monthly billing based on hourly rates, as well as fixed fee arrangements with and without reimbursement of specific expenses.

There are many other options, such as cost-plus-percentage contracts. In that type of contract, the consultant is paid all of the costs involved in the project plus some percentage of that as a fee.

A different arrangement may pay the consultant a per-

(Continued)

(Continued)

centage of the money the consultant saves or recaptures for the client. In both of these cases, the contract should define *precisely* the basis on which the consultant's compensation is being calculated. With the cost-plus contract, which costs are included and which excluded? Under the recapture approach, how will the parties calculate the money saved, and over what period of time? The money saved by a client can be evaluated daily, monthly, weekly, yearly, or longer. Needless to say, the period of time over which savings are measured will radically affect the consultant's compensation.

Anyone using any clause or document anywhere in this book should feel free to make every change needed so that the language accurately reflects the parties' intentions. The language of a contract contains no magic. It does reflect the accumulated experience of businesses, lawyers, and the courts. The key is clarity of expression. If the parties to a contract want different or additional provisions, they should not hesitate to include them. The only test should be that the clause reflects the rights and responsibilities of the parties to the contract *and* can be understood by a third party.

In sum, *the contract is both an expression of the agreement of the parties and a true management tool.* A well-drawn contract should eliminate problems, not cause them. There is an old saying among corporation lawyers that if a contract has to be interpreted by a court, then someone made a mistake in drafting it. This saying reflects the commercial reality that a well-drafted contract that memorializes negotiations between the parties and covers all facets of the relationship will lead to an effective, efficient performance of services on both sides. It will also minimize the likelihood that the parties ever will suffer a dispute.

NOTES

1. Sugata Biswas and Daryl Twichell, *Management Consulting: A Complete Guide to the Industry* (New York: Wiley, 1999), 7.

2. The Big Five are Anderson Consulting, Deloitte Consulting, Ernst & Young, KPMG Consulting, and PriceWaterhouse-Coopers.

3. Lewis Pinault, "Injecting Life into the Big 5," *Upside,* June 2000, 70, 77.

4. Pinault, "Injecting Life into the Big 5," 70.

5. Peter Galuszka, "Just-in-Time Manufacturing Is Working Overtime," *Business Week,* November 8, 1999, 36–37.

6. *Merriam-Webster Online Collegiate Dictionary,* 2000, s.v. "consult," http://www.aol.com (December 20, 2000).

7. *Merriam-Webster Online Collegiate Dictionary,* s.v. "consultant."

8. Biswas and Twichell, *Management Consulting,* 6.

9. Carol Hildebrand, "Walk the Walk," *CIO Magazine,* October 15, 1998, http://www.cio.com (September 28, 2000).

10. Attorney for plaintiffs in employment dispute with Microsoft, as quoted in Aaron Bernstein, "Temp Wars: Why Microsoft May Cry Uncle," *Business Week,* November 15, 1999, 48.

11. IRS Publication 15a, *Employer's Supplemental Tax Guide* (1999).

12. IRS Publication 15, *Circular E, Employer's Tax Guide* (1999).

13. Aaron Bernstein, "More Temp Trouble at Microsoft," *Business Week,* November 8, 1999, 6.

14. "Contractor Boomerang," *CFO,* July 1999, 14.

15. Portions of this are based on IRS Publication 15a, *Employer's Supplemental Tax Guide* (1999), portions of which are included in the Appendix B.

16. Sheila Seifert, "Hired Guns," December 20, 1999, http://www.officecom (December 20, 1999).

17. Seifert, "Hired Guns."

18. See, e.g., Catherine Arnold, "The Internal Consulting Practice of Strategic Planning," in Biswas and Twichell, *Management Consulting,* 79–86.

19. Travel consultant Michael Whitesage, "Working with Consultants," http://www.prismgrp.com (Jan. 25, 2000).

20. Ciddie Geddes, "How to Get the Expertise You Lack without Stressing Your Bottom Line," *Nevada Business Journal,* n.d., http://www.nevadabusiness.com (January 25, 2000).

21. Anonymous, "Confessions of an Ex-Consultant," *Fortune,* October 14, 1996, 107, 112.

22. Anonymous, "Confessions of an Ex-Consultant," 107, 108.

23. James O'Shea and Charles Madigan, *Dangerous Company: Management Consultants and the Businesses They Save and Ruin* (New York: Penguin Books, 1998), 302–303.

3

THE PAPER TRAIL: CORPORATE POLICIES

The consulting relationship is one shrouded in paper. In this and the next chapter, we deal with all the paper that makes up or has an impact on that relationship, with the exception of the final report or other product delivered by the consultant.

- At the relationship's beginning, or more correctly, *before* the beginning, come any written policies dealing with consultants—when they can be hired, what they can do, and how they are limited.
- Then come the various documents that the client and the consultant may use to try to define the project and the relationship—the Request for Quotation (RFQ), Request for Proposal (RFP), and the consultant proposal.
- Following that comes the contract. This may be one formal document, created by the client or consultant

or both, memorializing the relationship. Or it may be made up of a collection of papers, ranging from initial proposals to written work orders.
- Finally, there is the purchase order and the problem of determining where that document stands in the midst of the consulting relationship.

WHY HAVE A WRITTEN POLICY ON CONSULTANTS?

One of the biggest problems businesses face with regard to consultants is controlling their hiring and use. Many clients have no formal policy in that regard usually because consultants can be used in so many different areas that management never perceives the need for an overall policy.

But with no policy, a client has no real before-the-fact control, except indirect budgetary control, over the services consultants provide. Without such preexisting control, a client can neither ensure that it is using its consultants most effectively nor adequately protect its own interests in such vital areas as trade secrets.

With a policy, a client has control. In fact, *the very process of creating a policy is both an assertion of control and an exercise in sound management.* In creating a policy, management is forced to decide:

- What consultants can do for the business;
- What they should do for the business;
- What problems they might cause to or for the business; and
- How they should be retained by various parts of the business.

A formal, written policy is better than an "understood," unwritten policy for several reasons:

- An understood policy can, and usually does, become misunderstood over time. This happens through

40

misinterpretation as well as because of mistakes in transmitting its substance to new managers.

- A written policy can be reviewed by all affected managers *before* it is put in place and thus is more likely to meet their needs.
- A written policy can be modified more efficiently than one that is merely understood. As the military saying goes: "There is always someone who doesn't get the word."

A written policy does not have to mean that consultants will be hired and managed uniformly. Rather, it should at least permit uniform retention and management standards and procedures.

WHAT SHOULD A COMPANY POLICY ON CONSULTANTS COVER?

Admittedly, every client has a different approach to corporate policies, but each should consider preparing a policy on the use and retention of outside consultants. The contents of a company policy on consultants should reflect the structure and operation of the client's organization.

Just as with the consulting relationship itself, there is no such thing as a standard consulting policy. The policy will reflect unique conditions, such as decentralized versus centralized management. However, a basic company policy should cover at least the following topics:

- Who or what has the responsibility for preparing and keeping current the procedures that govern the retention and use of outside consultants and consulting services?
- Are there overall limitations on the proper use of consultants? For example, is their use counted against personnel limits for certain purposes?

- Is prior approval required to hire a consultant? If so, in what circumstances, and by whom?

If you, as the client, see that your firm has a history of duplicative consulting engagements or has faced problems with badly negotiated agreements, you may want to consider establishing an internal consulting manager, or at least an internal consulting information center. That could deal with issues such as these:

- Does anyone know what kinds of projects are currently under way in-house at one time, to avoid redundancy?
- Is there one person or a small group who is particularly skilled at negotiating consulting contracts? Should that person or group do that, or merely provide guidance?
- What about assigning an internal manager to each consulting retention to serve as a watchdog for corporate interests? Such interests can range from ensuring compliance with travel policies to ensuring that a particular consultant does not cause employee morale problems.

Additional questions often addressed in written policies on the retention and use of outside consultants include the following:

- Are consultants required to be bound by any other of the client's policies, such as those regarding travel or communication with competitors?
- Should the final report from every consulting project be sent to a particular individual in the client organization? If so, why?
- Should there be a system for standardized review of the performance of outside consultants? Where should such evaluations be sent? Who else can use them? Is their use mandatory?

- In very large enterprises, should a consultant be asked to disclose if it is doing similar work elsewhere for the client? Should the client have to disclose if similar work is also being done for it by other consultants?
- If prior approval of the retention of a consultant is not needed, should the unit retaining a consultant have to report that retention to a third party? If so, why?
- Are there separate budget controls over the use of consulting services? What are they, and why are they in place?

Coverage

The first problem to address in establishing a corporate policy on the hiring of outside consultants is to specify exactly what outside consultants are. This is directly related to the kind of control the client wishes to exercise over the use of consultants in its organization. In the sample corporate policy text shown here, the drafters use a generally accepted definition of outside consultants.

Definition: Outside consultants provide personal and professional services of a purely advisory nature, such as the development of policy. They do *not* perform operating functions or supervise those functions. Outside consultants' services include advice about management and administration; these services do not include commercial and industrial services or research. The services of outside consultants are provided by persons and firms generally considered to have expertise, knowledge, and ability of particular value to a Division.

But as with all such definitions, this one includes certain policy judgments. For example, by defining a consultant as one who does not perform or supervise operating functions, this client bars any outside consultant from carrying out such duties. But it is not improbable that a consultant may be hired, in part, to supervise operating functions. In fact, the federal government is often criticized for using outside consultants and contractors in this way. In addition, some properly calling themselves consultants perform what may be described as research services on a contract basis. If a client believes it will be retaining consultants for such services, it should include those services in the definition and thus in the policy's coverage.

Note that if a function is not included in the corporate policy's definition of consulting, then a consultant could be hired but not be subject to other restrictions of the client's overall policy. For example, if the policy requires prior approval to hire consultants, but the definition of consulting excludes research services, a consultant doing research could be hired without prior approval.

Directional Policy

The next step in creating the corporate policy is drafting a decentralized or directional policy. Such a policy requires each division to prepare its own procedures and guidelines concerning the retention of outside consultants, based on a broad directive in the overall policy. This approach is particularly useful in an organization whose various divisions have different consultant needs—for example, engineering consultants in one division, marketing consultants for another, and compensation specialists for a third. The guidelines in paragraph 1 of the policy statement are designed to reflect this. A smaller or more centralized client may wish to adopt paragraph 1 as a directive without more detail.

The retention and use of consultants is often subject to both budget and contract review, at least for agreements for services in excess of a fixed amount. Including such information in the written direction assures the client that its procedures are being followed, particularly that the terms of the consulting agreement, the description of the services to be rendered, and the total compensation are defined clearly in advance. In addition, legal review may be required for all consulting relationships covering services performed for longer than a period of one year, if for no other reason than the statute of frauds applies. The paragraph shown here is designed to ensure that such review is obtained:

Each Division issues procedures, to be approved by [name of office which approves such policies], that require that:

a. Every requirement for outside consultants be justified in writing;

b. Agreements with outside consultants be complete and specify a fixed period of performance for the services to be provided; and

c. Legal and budget review be completed for all agreements for services in excess of one year or costing more than $25,000.

Overall Limitations on the Use of Consultants

An alternative approach is to limit those situations where outside consultants properly may be used, as has been done in the sample policy statement that follows:

Outside consultants may be used by Divisions only when:

a. Specialized opinions or professional or technical advice is required and is not available within the Corporation;

(Continued)

45

(Continued)

b. An outside point of view on a critical issue is necessary;
c. State-of-the-art knowledge, education, or research is needed;
d. An opinion of a noted expert with national or international prestige is essential to the success of a key project; or
e. Services of special personnel who are not needed full-time or cannot serve full-time are required.

The definitions in this sample are general but permit senior management some indirect control over the use of consultants. If this statement of policy were coupled with the definition of consulting given earlier, in light of the comments prohibiting outside consultants from making management decisions or bypassing or undermining personnel limits, more detailed requirements may be counterproductive.

Requiring Prior Approval

If prior approval of some sort is desirable, then the following paragraph can be used. It is designed to ensure that operating managers cannot retain consultants without approval from at least one senior layer of management.

Each Division establishes specific levels of delegations of authority to approve the use of outside consultants. At least [number] levels of approval are required to hire an outside consultant. [You can add additional limits, such as that this applies only to contracts longer than six months, or for more than $25,000, etc.]

Requiring prior approval may be desirable for one or more reasons:

- It can force managers to articulate more completely the reason for using consultants and the reasons for selecting a particular consultant.
- It permits review of the decision to hire a consultant to determine if the terms of retention are consistent with the client's budget and legal policies.
- It allows senior management to suggest consideration of alternative methods of accomplishing the same result. It also allows senior management to suggest alternative consultants for consideration, including other consultants already working for the client in related areas. This should not be the same as requiring such changes.

A client's policy, of course, may require that only one particular person or one particular unit be authorized to retain consultants; or it could provide that such an office must merely review the retention of consultants where the contract will involve more than a predetermined amount of money.

HOW EXISTING CORPORATE POLICIES AFFECT YOUR USE OF CONSULTANTS

Without overstating it, there is virtually no corporate policy that does not have some impact, direct or indirect, on either the retention of or utilization of outside consultants under some circumstances. For example, a corporate policy on reimbursement for travel and entertainment expenses may, according to its terms, apply only to employees. Yet sound management prescribes that it probably should also apply to consultants, for several good reasons:

- The policy establishes a complete set of standards to deal with a recurring situation.
- The policy may reflect tax considerations, so that all reimbursements will be tax deductible for the client.
- It may damage morale for employees to know or even suspect, for example, that consultants can travel first class while they cannot under the same conditions.

In general, you should review all of your current corporate policies to determine the following:

- Do the policies clearly apply to, or exclude, outside consultants? If they do not apply, should they? How? If they seem to apply, should consultants be exempted from their coverage?
- Should the policies be modified to reflect the fact that the status of the consultant differs in important ways when compared with that of your employees?
- How can consultants be made aware of the existence, limits, and application of company policies to their work for you? Are they being informed of such policies now?

You should do the review whether or not you elect to develop a separate policy on consultants. You may find that merely modifying some company policies to cover (or exclude) consultants will limit what you need in a formal policy on consultants. It may even eliminate the need for such a policy.

There are a number of areas in which practical experience has shown that the corporation should consider establishing new or amending existing corporate policies to address the issues raised by the retention and use of consultants. Here are the ones most often overlooked:

- Finder's fees.
- Outside independent public accountants.

- Outside legal counsel and lobbyists.
- Risk management.
- Insider trading.
- Foreign Corrupt Practices Act.
- Employee references and records.

Finder's Fees

Some clients have no written policy for dealing with finder's fees in conjunction with mergers and acquisitions; instead they rely on an oral policy or set of standards. Many merger and acquisition transactions today are conducted with the assistance of business-merger consultants specifically retained by the client. Such consultants advise clients on potential acquisitions, suggest possible merger targets, and evaluate the pros and cons of potential deals. They also may directly assist in the negotiations leading to an acquisition. For these specialized services they may be paid a fixed fee, an hourly rate, a contingent fee based on the acquisition price, or some combination thereof.

There are also business-merger consultants who try to broker acquisitions on a freelance basis. Known as "finders," they approach potential merger partners suggesting that a particular company is a good takeover target. Some of these business brokers or merger consultants may perform a useful service for a client by identifying future investments. Those who act as finders will claim a fee by reason of the existence of an implied or oral contract with the client to which they provided the information. A difficult problem can arise in cases where such information is unsolicited *and* there is no subsequent written agreement between the finder and the client; the finder, if his or her information materially contributed to the merger or acquisition, may still be entitled to a fee, even without a formal agreement.

There have been and will continue to be disputes over such fees, both with established business-consulting firms as well as those often described as "bucket shop" or "fly-by-night" operators. The latter are characterized by a technique that often consists of sending letters, or even messages by e-mail, to executives of corporations suggesting a particular company as a target for takeover. If the corporation eventually does acquire the target company, the broker will present himself or herself and demand a fee for services rendered. The corporation may find itself in the position of having to pay such a fee when in fact it did not use the information if, for example, the information was sent to an executive who promptly disposed of it and the corporation cannot show that it did not rely on that material. Such disputes are extremely sensitive matters. Their sensitivity arises from several factors, not the least of which is that the size of the fee in question, in the case of a major acquisition, can be quite large.

To defend the case, the client may have to disclose in court its merger strategy and the sources of its merger advice. Moreover, the client may have to prove a negative—that it did not use the information it actually received. Therefore, a company actively involved in acquisitions or mergers should have a written policy concerning finder's fees. Such a policy should deal both with the retention of business brokers and with the handling of unsolicited pieces of information dealing with such opportunities. In particular, the policy should attempt to assist employees in identifying exactly when a person is acting as a merger or business broker to protect the company from future liability. Although no policy can stop unsolicited proposals from being made, it can establish procedures to minimize their impact; further, it should limit who retains legitimate brokers.

These procedures should also require that all unsolicited proposals be forwarded to some central location or person. If the employee receiving such materials can identify a mailing as a potential proposal (by the return address, for example), he or she should forward it, unopened. In all other cases, it should be read only enough to identify the subject matter and then forwarded on. No copies should be made along the way; only a record of its transmittal should be kept. In addition, the person to whom such materials are sent should not be one with responsibilities in the merger and acquisition area, so there can be no question of his or her misuse merely by reading it.

The entire proposal should be returned to the sender by certified mail, return receipt requested, with a cover letter noting that it was unsolicited and no copy has been made. No copy should be kept of the proposal, only of the cover letter, and the cover letter should not make reference to specifics of the contents of the proposal. If desired, the company can also advise the sender on how to formally submit a proposal.

Outside Independent Public Accountants

Corporations increasingly have written policies dealing with their relations with their outside independent public accountants, that is, the firms responsible for auditing their books and records. Some major accounting firms reportedly prefer that all contact with them, audit and nonaudit alike, from public companies in particular, be made by or through one client officer. Generally they are more concerned about nonaudit services than about those requested by the board of directors and management for a company's financial reports to the U.S. Securities and Exchange Commission (SEC), stock exchanges, and shareholders. The SEC requires that firms operating as independent auditors disclose the nature and extent of nonaudit services provided to their clients, so that the shareholders and the public can evaluate if the independence of the auditors has been compromised.

This is a consulting-related issue, for the major (and increasingly, medium-sized) accounting firms also provide management consulting services, as well as other types of nonaccounting services, such as personnel and information technology consulting services. The concern from the company's point of view is that, for example, a request for the consulting arm of the accounting firm to establish cash management procedures in a particular subsidiary could constitute a conflict for the main accounting firm. The firm could be placing its auditor in the position of having to audit its own audit or evaluate the efficiency and security of procedures that another part of it developed.

To avoid such potential conflicts, the client should take its own steps and not rely on the procedures established by its accountants to prevent them. That means a company should establish internal procedures by first identifying its independent auditors and then either prohibiting their use for any other purpose except an audit or by requiring that *all requests* for their use be processed through one corporate officer. This officer could be the one with whom the accounting firm works most frequently, such as the chief financial officer, or it could be the officer who supervises the client's reports to the SEC, or both. The best situation is that regardless of through whom such requests are processed, both persons know of the request. The policy should clearly provide that no retention of any part of the identified auditing firm can be approved or initiated without this prior review and approval. There should be no exceptions to this policy.

Outside Legal Counsel and Lobbyists

Although not arising as frequently as the question of the employment of the independent auditors in other capacities, some review should be made of any policies on the retention of outside legal counsel. Outside legal counsel may serve in a quasi-consulting capacity to a client. If a client hires lawyers just to provide advice and not appear in court or before a judicial agency, they are really serving in a consulting relationship. Advice rendered by lawyers that may put them in a consulting relationship includes the following:

- Designing employee benefit packages, a service also performed by accounting and actuarial firms.
- Advising on mergers and acquisitions, a service also performed by merger consultants and investment bankers.
- Reviewing consumer complaint or employee grievance systems, a service also performed by corporate communications consultants.

The overlap in some areas of practice between the accounting and legal disciplines is so profound that the major accounting firms are openly seeking ways in which they can engage in the practice of law.

Occasionally, outside attorneys in turn hire specialist attorneys to provide unusual or very narrowly applicable advice to the law firm. This often happens in areas that traditionally have been legal specialties, such as admiralty or patent law. In these cases, the firm's own lawyers are hiring consultants. Thus, their retention should be governed by the client's policies, which in turn should be applied to outside counsel for several reasons:

- The lawyers are hiring another person who also may properly hold himself or herself out as a representative of the client. There are remote chances that this could expose the client to additional liability.
- The client should be aware that the lawyers it has hired do not have the needed expertise and must seek outside aid.
- The client may wish to exercise direct control over the legal (and, by implication, other) consultants its own lawyers hire and whom it ultimately must pay.
- The client may find that its reputation is affected by association with these consultants and thus should

exercise some say in their initial and ultimate utilization.

Some lawyers are lobbyists, but not all lobbyists are lawyers. The use of lobbyists is particularly sensitive, as they are consultants, and all the controls and contractual issues surrounding the retention and use of outside consultants apply to them. In addition, lobbyists represent the client in the political arena. The power to retain them should be limited to a small number of senior executives, and they should be subject to continual supervision. The supervision should require:

- Prompt registration of all lobbyists working on behalf of the client, if required by law (some state and federal laws require both the lobbyist and the retaining client to register if legislative lobbying is being conducted);
- Careful, ongoing review of all lobbyist expenditures (lobbyists often have been viewed as conduits for "payoffs" to public officials, either directly or through excessive spending or entertaining); and
- Disclosure of the exact nature of the relationship, if any, between a client's political action committee and its lobbyists.

Risk Management

The important field of corporate risk management now encompasses not merely the purchase of insurance but also loss control and the management of claims, as well as the ongoing analysis of and mitigation of risks. Corporations who have adopted or will adopt formal written policies on corporate risk management should always remember that the retention of consultants is a matter of some interest to a risk management officer, at least from a risk policy point of view. For example, a risk management officer may wish to verify that all insurance issues raised in the consulting agreement are resolved. Examples of such issues are the retaining of "key man" insurance on a consultant whose project is absolutely vital to the client or the client requiring the consultant to show proof of any coverage (such as workers' compensation insurance) that the consultant legally is required to have. How the review is conducted is a matter for the risk management officer to determine. But once written policies are adopted, they should cover the retention of outside consultants.

Insider Trading

Prompted by federal and state securities laws, clients with publicly listed stock have adopted formal written policies dealing with transactions of their own stocks and bonds. Such policies are designed to prevent the improper use of "inside information" by their employees. They often also deal with reporting purchases and sales by officers and directors when they are not acting on inside information. Although the law, as interpreted by the SEC and the federal courts, does not directly include consultants as "insiders" subject to the requirements and penalties of federal securities law, clients with publicly traded securities will do well to think about this issue. More and more, the legal system tends to track down where such information has traveled and who profited from it. So it is probably very desirable to require that consultants be made aware of the client's policies in this regard. In fact, a statement in their contracts that the consultants are aware of these policies, as suggested in the sample policy language on page 56, may be of assistance here. It may be advisable to require that the corporate policy on using inside knowledge apply not only to employees and their families but also to individuals serving in a consulting relationship with the client who have access to particularly sensitive nonpublic information.

Employee References and Records

The number of state and federal laws dealing, directly or indirectly, with employee records and references continues to increase. These laws mean that most clients have written guidelines governing the retention of employee records as well as whether, how, and when they give references on former or current employees to third parties. In formulating such policies, a client should consider whether its policy should cover providing references on consultants, both individual and corporate, that it has retained in the past.

ADHERING TO CORPORATE POLICIES

Having reviewed which policies have an impact on your use of consultants, you may also want to determine which policies should be followed by your consultants. To accomplish this on the broadest possible scale, you can use the following policy statement:

Every outside consultant must agree, in writing, to be bound by the corporation's policies.

This may sound like a "motherhood" statement, but it is important to consider. By requiring a consultant to be bound by the client's corporate policies, the client at least can assure itself that the consultant understands the scope of the client's position on critical topics ranging from business ethics to conflicts of interest. In addition, it enables the client to subject a consultant and the retention to a wide variety of administrative and budgetary policies, such as restrictions on travel expenditures, without having to repeat them in the consultant policy or in the consulting agreement. Of course, to be bound, the consultant must be given a copy of the policies. In addition, if the policies might have any impact on the retention, the consultant should at least be told what they are, so that any quotation or proposal can take them into account. In fact, it is probably preferable that a consultant that is ready to provide a quote or proposal should *see* all of the policies that will apply to it before getting to pricing.

However, the client should be quite sure that it wants the consultant bound by all of the client's policies. If the client has some doubt, then the particular policies that are binding must be spelled out.

Every outside consultant must agree, in writing, to be bound by the corporation's policies on travel, conflicts of interest, and handling confidential information.

Consultants, too, are concerned about client policies that might have an impact on their performance and, particularly, their pricing. Some use a clause like the following one in their formal proposals to get from the client copies of any such policies. The second sentence protects the consultant by giving it the right to reprice or even withdraw from the retention if it is presented with policies that make its performance too costly or even impossible.

Client policies: The Client has provided/will provide/has not provided the Consultant with copies of any policies or procedures applicable to this Assignment. The Client specifically agrees that if any of these policies or procedures should materially impact the way in which the Consultant will conduct the Assignment, the Consultant has the right to reprice this Assignment or to withdraw from this Assignment without penalty.

4

THE PAPER TRAIL: CONTRACTING ISSUES

A consulting agreement may have to cover many of the same elements found in the traditional employment contract as well as independent contractor elements appropriate to the client-consultant relationship. These elements are dealt with here because they need to be considered in virtually every consulting agreement. But they are only the starting point. The contractual issues raised by the creation of and management of the consulting relationship will be covered throughout this book.

> "Carefully crafted contracts do . . . play an important role in outsourcing, but experienced managers know their limitations and the importance of mutual adaptation to omissions, unanticipated project-threatening obstacles, new opportunities, and new requirements that emerge during the [project contracted for]."[1]

WHY THE CONSULTING RELATIONSHIP SHOULD BE IN A WRITTEN CONTRACT

Regardless of the duration of the retention, the kind of services provided, or the compensation paid, no consulting relationship should be entered into without some kind of written agreement. Why? There are both legal and management reasons:

- From a legal standpoint, certain agreements cannot be enforced at all without some written documents that constitute evidence of the agreement between the parties. Examples of this are agreements relating to real property, agreements to be performed over a long period of time, and agreements that involve payment upon the occurrence of certain contingencies.
- From a management standpoint, without a written document between the parties indicating the nature of the services to be performed, the parties simply are asking for trouble. Even assuming that an agreement has been entered into in good faith, good faith at the beginning does not prevent intervening problems or events. Memories are not infallible, and one person's recollection of a conversation may not be the same as someone else's.
- Another, more common management problem that can arise in a retention based on an oral agreement concerns the services to be provided. Suppose, for example, that an officer of a client retains a consultant orally. Over the course of the project, the consultant receives differing instructions from the officer who hired the firm, from officers and employees with whom the consultant is working, and from the hiring officer's superiors. Is the consultant to treat these directions as modifications in the contract? Or do they constitute a new contract between the consultant and the client? Is the consultant to disregard some or all of them? Which ones? This is

just one example of what can happen when the consulting relationship is oral only.

Throughout the model legal clauses, we call the parties "the Client" and "the Consultant." *In drafting an agreement, the client should never be called "the Employer," as even the use of that term could undermine the independent contractor status of the consultant.*

WHAT MAKES UP THE CONTRACT?

The contract between the client and the consultant can be a single document or it can be a collection of documents. If it is one document, such as a written proposal offered by the consultant and signed by the client, then the terms of the contract are determined by what is in the writing. If the parties have agreed on other terms, a court will enforce the written document first and will consider the oral (nonwritten) terms only in two situations:

1. The oral terms cover matters not covered by the written document; or
2. The oral terms cover matters in the written document and the court can be convinced that both parties intended that the contract be modified by their oral agreements *and* the contract does not contain a statement (the so-called integration clause) to the effect that it contains the entire agreement between the parties.

This document contains the entire agreement between

(Continued)

(Continued)

the Client and the Consultant. It cannot be amended or modified orally, but only by a written document, signed by both parties [alternative: signed by the party against whom the enforcement of any amendment or modification is sought].

At this point, sound management dictates that the parties entering into the agreement really have incorporated all of their understandings, terms, and conditions in the document. If the document does not contain the entire agreement of the parties, it should be revised. The second sentence of the sample text protects both parties against oral modification, that is, changing the written document by nonwritten means. In the case of the consultant, it avoids the problem that can arise from dealing with several people at the corporate level who may be giving contradictory or new instructions for assignments not covered by the agreement. In the case of the client, it protects against misunderstandings with the consultant and ensures that the instructions given to the consultant are thought out fully and are within the bounds of the agreement.

However, no matter how hard the parties try, the relationship may not be encompassed within one single document. So the parties should be aware that a contract can also be made up of a series of written documents. For example, following signing a contract, the client may want the delivery date changed. If the consultant agrees, the two parties should sign, or at least initial, a document that notes the change. Then, the contract between the parties is contained (memorialized) in two documents, the second of which amends the first.

Another example is the case where the contract covers a wide range of services, and the client wants to be able to add to or make changes in specific projects within agreed-upon limits. A similar situation can arise where the consultant is retained for a long period of time and the client wants to be able to use the consultant's services as the need arises. In these situations, the contract should provide that the client has the right to order changes in the work. *Remember that as an independent contractor, the consultant cannot be told by the client how to do its work, but only what to do.* In these cases, the contract should provide a way for the changes or additions to be handled so that they are captured in writing for the protection of both sides. It should also provide that the work in progress will not be affected.

The Consultant will perform [describe the assignment]. These services to be performed by the Consultant may be changed by the Client from time to time by letter requests [work order, change orders] sent to you by [name of authorized person].

In these cases, the contract now is made up of the original document plus all the additions and changes, sometimes known as work orders, change orders, or letter requests.

The last situation we'll consider is when the parties have exchanged a series of documents but have not taken the time to put them all together. For example, the client may have sent a consultant a letter asking for a quote or proposal for work on a particular project. The letter was preceded by a confidentiality agreement, which the client required that the consultant sign, so that the client could share confidential information needed to prepare a response.

The consultant then replies, using the consultant's own form, which adds language dealing with billing and payment terms (10 days net) as well as language dealing with confidentiality. The client sends the consultant a message via e-mail, telling the consultant to proceed, a purchase order is being prepared, and the consultant should use a certain PO number on invoices. In the midst of working on the retention, the consultant gets the PO, which contains information on billing, noting that all bills are 60 days net.

What is the contract here? Unfortunately, because the parties have not made clear what they intended with each step, two courts looking at this might come to different conclusions. In this case, the agreement between the two parties would *probably* include the following:

- The confidentiality agreement signed at the beginning.
- The project description set forth in the client letter. If the proposal changed what the letter said, that change would probably be allowed as a part of the final agreement.
- The terms in the proposal, with the exception of the confidentiality language. If that merely supplemented and expanded on what the consultant signed, a court would probably consider it an amendment. However, if it was less strict than that sent out by the client, problems might arise. One view would be that the first confidentiality clause vanished and was replaced by the new one, as the client accepted the proposal as offered. An equally valid alternative is that this clause is an offer of an amendment to the confidentiality agreement. Because there could be a question whether an e-mail message is a document "signed" by the client approving an amendment, this could be up in the air.

The last issue is whether the payment terms in the proposal apply or the ones in the PO do. If the consultant never saw the PO before starting, it could argue that the client cannot amend the terms of the agreement after accepting them and allowing the consultant to start. An equally valid argument can be made that, as the consultant knew that the client used a PO, it was obligated to check whether that differed from its proposal offer.

Regardless of the outcome, one thing is clear: When the parties do not incorporate all the elements in one place and a dispute arises, it will be up to someone else to determine what is the actual agreement between the parties. And the parties may be very surprised by the result.

Request for Proposal

Request for Proposal (RFP) is usually used when a client has already determined exactly what it needs done, at least in terms of the end result desired. The client describes in detail the results desired, provides information about its business and other items, outlines terms governing the way in which the project will be managed, and asks for a response. The response to an RFP is a document in which the consultant typically provides the following:

- A description of the qualifications and skills the consultant will bring to the assignment. While this is typically not always explicitly required, most experienced consultants include it on the basis that the proposal may be reviewed by persons unfamiliar with them.
- A statement of what the consultant intends to do, and how it will approach the project.
- Information on the individual or individuals who would work on the project.
- Special terms that are part of the offer, including payment terms, prepayments, requirements for on-site facilities, client cooperation, and the like.
- Pricing on the project. This may be a fixed price, an estimate of low/high costs, an hourly rate or rates with estimates of hours to be utilized, details on costs, and so on. The goal is to allow the client to determine the likely total cost of the retention.

A client then reviews all the proposals it receives. It may have asked only one firm to provide a proposal, or the RFP may have been widely distributed. That is the client's option. Then, based on a review of the responding proposals, the client awards the retention to one firm. In a few cases, a client may go back to one or two finalists and ask that they repropose. But this is a costly step for the consultants and a time-consuming one for the client, so it should rarely be done. It should go without saying that unless those responding to the RFP are told in advance that their response may be shared with competitors, a client should never show a response from one firm to another.

RFPs include a response date after which proposals will not be accepted. Some RFPs provide that a proposal must stay open for a fixed period. In all cases, the time frames should be reasonable. If you request a response to an RFP in a relatively short period of time, you should be prepared to respond equally rapidly and not require that proposals be kept open for an excessive period of time.

The final terms of the agreement between the client and the consultant are typically made up of the terms included in the RFP. To that are added, first, the pricing and other customized responses from the consultant, second, any new terms and conditions advanced by the consultant, and third, any changes in the terms requested by the client. To avoid pasting together such an agreement, experienced clients provide in the RFP that on acceptance, all of the terms and conditions will be incorporated into one final document. Taking this approach allows both sides to make sure that they understand what the client has agreed to and what it will hold firm on.

Request for Quotation

Technically, the Request for Quotation (RFQ) should be a document that sets forth, in detail, what the client needs done, what it expects a consultant to do, and all terms and conditions, such as payment, indemnification, insurance, and so on, that will apply to the retention. It is sent to firms that have been precleared as qualified for the retention. In that way, a responding firm merely sends in pricing information. As with the RFP, that may be a fixed price, an hourly rate, or some other option. Typically, the terms of the RFQ require that the pricing be kept firm for a set period of time.

When the client decides, it notifies the winning firm. The decision should be based on pricing alone, as all firms have already been prequalified. Usually, the winning firm just signs a contract, which was a part of the RFQ, and can begin.

Some clients erroneously label an RFP as an RFQ. This happens most often in cases where the client has a fairly detailed statement of its needs, and even of deliverables, but is asking for information about a firm's qualifications in addition to its pricing. Implicit in this is that the decision is to be made on price and qualifications. Properly, a process that asks for anything more than pricing and related terms is not an RFQ.

Before drafting that RFP or RFQ, stop! Ask yourself *who* should be doing this. For example, if you are planning to ask only one consultant for a proposal for a retention, consider asking that consultant to *help you* draft a statement of the scope of the work. That way both of you are, literally, on the same page when the retention goes forward.

On the other hand, if you plan to ask several consultants to propose for a retention, consider two preliminary options:

- First, you may want each of the candidates to provide comments and questions to you in the form of a draft proposal, one without costs or fee data or estimates. Look-

(Continued)

(Continued)

ing at the draft proposals will allow you to identify problems in the retention, as well as to articulate more precisely what it is you want and need—and what you do not want or need. In addition, this may let you test whether your expectations about what the retention can accomplish are realistic. While some consultants may decline to help out in this proposal development process, most will because it allows the consultant to demonstrate its expertise in addition to the way that it can master the requirements.

- Second, you may wish to retain a firm to help you draft the RFP/RFQ and help you evaluate it. This firm is, of course, to be excluded from competing for the assignment. It is hired as much for its knowledge of your firm as for its knowledge of the area under consideration. But in areas where the technical expertise and experience of the consultant is difficult to evaluate yet critical to the assignment, this additional small expenditure may avoid a large mistake.

Consultant Proposals

In the course of developing a relationship, a consultant may submit an unsolicited proposal to a client. Alternatively, a client, following discussions with a consultant, may ask the consultant for a "proposal on this." In either case, the client should exercise great care in properly handling such a document.

- First, if the proposal is unsolicited and the client does not want to consider it, it should be returned as quickly as possible to the consultant.
- Second, if the proposal is of any interest, the client should quickly review it for anything that it must

68

deal with up front. For example, if the proposal expires shortly and the client would like more time to review it, that should be handled at once. In addition, if all discussions must be under a confidentiality agreement, that should be drafted, sent out, and returned before reviewing the document.

- Third, the client should review the document very carefully. Is it responsive? Are the terms clear? If any points need clarification, those changes should be made in writing.
- Fourth, if standard terms apply to all contracts for consulting services or if the consultant services will be governed by a purchase order, the client should get those to the consultant now, if they were not provided earlier. The consultant should be given the opportunity to revise the proposal in light of any of these new terms or conditions.
- Fifth, the proposal should never be shown to any firm in competition for the same retention, nor should it be used as the basis for soliciting proposals from other firms. If a client needs significant assistance in soliciting proposals or developing an RFP, it should retain those services, and not exploit the work put into developing a proposal by a consultant without competition.
- Sixth, if the proposal is acceptable, the client should take care in communicating that. If there are no changes needed, the client should state that. If the proposal is acceptable but only with changes, the client must not say the proposal has been approved. It should say it can be approved if certain changes are made. Once the changes have been made, then, and only then, should the client accept it.
- Seventh, if the proposal is not acceptable, the client should either inform the consultant of that on a timely basis or ask for a new proposal, pointing out what else it wants or needs.

- Eighth, the client should be prompt. If a proposal is not satisfactory, it should get that message out. If the client solicited a proposal with a very short turnaround time, it should be prepared to respond equally quickly. *One rule of thumb is that you should take no longer to respond to a proposal you solicited than you gave the firm to work on it.* So if a client asks for a proposal (whether competitively on not) to be completed in five business days, it should be prepared to give the consultant a decision in five business days from the time it receives the proposal.

Some consultants rely on standard or sample forms provided by their professional and trade organizations. In making them available to their members, such organizations suggest that such forms provide their members a number of advantages, including the freedom to rely on carefully prepared language to define the relative responsibilities of the parties. If you can have access to these forms before negotiations begin, you can gain several key points:

- First, you will be aware that the consultant may propose that the relationship be entered into based upon this standard form.
- Second, if the consultant uses the standard form, you will already be familiar with it, having had time to review it.
- Third, if the consultant has developed its own form, that form likely will reflect many of the standard clauses from the organization's form.
- Fourth, by reviewing these contract forms you can evaluate your own standard agreement to determine whether there are problems unique to this type of consulting that should be reflected in your agreement. If so, you then have the opportunity to modify your agreement to make it apply more specifically to this type of consulting *before* enter-

ing into negotiations for the acquisition of consulting services.
- Finally, studying standard contract documents enables you to understand better how the consultants of that type work. And understanding how consultants work will enable you to deal with them and use their services more effectively once you have a contract with them.

From your point of view as the client, it can be useful to know that such contracts are provided to organization members even if they are not available to you as a nonmember. That is because this increases the likelihood that the consultant you may be dealing with will propose the organization's standard form contract as a beginning point. Even if you are not familiar with the contents of such form contracts, knowing that a standard form will be proposed can give you a perspective on the way to bargain over the terms of the agreement.

One way to handle problems created by the need for internal legal review of the terms offered by a consultant is to ask the consultant with whom you *may* work to provide you with its standard terms and conditions. Then "run these by" your legal department and get its feedback. Go over that with the consultants. Then when you are ready to use that firm you can give the legal department the terms of the particular engagement and remind them that the balance of the terms of the offer have already been cleared by them.

Core Contract Concepts

While every consulting relationship is different, when preparing a consulting contract, there are several core issues to resolve. They are not "boilerplate." Rather, by considering them, both the client and consultant begin the process of defining their relationship in the clearest possible manner.

Defined Terms

In a contract, the first time a specialized term is used, it can be followed by a word or phrase in parentheses or quotes. This is lawyers' shorthand, designed to handle the need to repeat a specific idea or name. As a matter of style, lawyers tend to capitalize such defined words to show throughout the agreement that they carry some special meaning. For example, once you have described the assignment, the parties could identify all that it entails by one term, such as the word *Work*. Then, every time that word is used, it describes that vast range of services.

Independent Contractor Status and Related Issues

As discussed earlier, the status of an independent contractor is the key legal element in the consulting relationship. For this reason, it should be dealt with in every agreement. *Merely stating in an agreement that the consultant's relationship to the client is that of an independent contractor does not create that relationship automatically. Such a statement is, however, a good starting place.*

When a client gives up the right to direct and control the consultant and the consultant's employees regarding the result to be accomplished and the manner and means by which that result is obtained, an independent contractor relationship is created. The client must always respect this allocation of control. That is because the creation and maintenance of the independent contractor relationship is determined both by the contract's language *and* the actual practice of the parties under that contract. If the client exercises direct control over the consultant and the consultant's employees, it may subject the client to liability for the torts of the consultant and its employees.

> Independent Contractor. You shall exercise control over the means and manner in which you perform any work requested hereunder, and in all respects your relationship to the Corporation shall be that of an independent contractor serving as a consultant, and not as an employee.

The following example is another way to express the consultant's status. One difference is that it also sets a standard of performance for the consultant—that is, the consultant will "use its best efforts." By agreeing to this, the consultant is not promising success, but rather that it will do its very best.

> Independent Contractor. The Consultant [will use its best efforts in carrying out this Assignment and] will retain control over the means and manner in which it performs this Assignment. In all respects, the Consultant's relationship to the Client is that of an independent contractor, not an employee.

Too many people mistakenly believe that using language such as this, whether it is followed or not, creates legal protection. That belief is wrong; this language only establishes the relationship between the parties. In order for a client to prove that its relationship with the consultant is that of a client and an independent contractor, the client must rely on the facts of the relationship. The sample paragraph tells the parties how they should treat each other; if they treat each other in this manner, the relationship will be that of an independent contractor.

The following paragraph is an expanded version of the previous one. Because the parties know that several of the consultant's employees will be involved in the retention, the clause now sets out the legal standards governing that type of relationship. Remember, it is not only the statement of the relationship that is important, but also the fact that the parties to the contract *adhere to* this distinction.

All employees of Consultant engaged in any of the Work [Work is a defined term, that is, what the Consultant will be doing for the Client] performed by the Consultant under this Contract shall be subject to the sole direction, supervision, and control of Consultant at all times and in all places. The Consultant shall exercise control over the means and manner in which it and its employees perform the Work requested by the Client under this Contract. In all respects Consultant's relationship and the relationship of all of Consultant's employees to the Client shall be that of an independent contractor.

Because the consultant is not an employee, the client does not have an automatic legal right to intellectual assets developed by the consultant during the retention. For that reason, the agreement should cover not only the ownership and disposition of any patentable or copyrightable work product but also the client's right to the consultant's work product, both during the term of the agreement and at its termination. In addition, the client may want to consider whether the agreement should cover work product that is not patentable or copyrightable as well as that which can be patented or copyrighted.

The importance of these clauses may be demonstrated by a federal contracting problem reported years ago in the *Washington Post*. To entice bidders, a federal agency seeking an outside evaluation of an experimental drug agreed that the consultant testing the drug would be able to exploit the drug commercially at the end of the contract. The contract provided that the consultant could keep the treatment records and use them in later seeking approval from the Food and Drug Administration to sell the drug. When the federal agency decided to terminate the project before it was completed, it learned that it was not entitled to any of the treatment records from the consultant, even though the consultant no longer could hope to market the drug. In essence, the agency had paid for research it would never get and no one would ever use.[2]

The following paragraph is designed to handle the development of patentable or copyrightable processes or techniques.

The Client shall have the right to and shall own any and all patentable or copyrightable inventions, processes, plans, or techniques, together with any applications for patents or copyrights and patents and the copyrights that may issue thereunder, which are created, developed, or invented by Consultant or any of its employees as a result of, or arising out of, the Work [a defined term, the retention for which the Consultant is being hired] under this Contract. At the Client's request and expense, Consultant agrees to do, or cause to be done, all things necessary to enable the Client to require the full right to the use and ownership of any and all the rights and properties described in this paragraph.

This language provides that the client will receive the benefits of the work product because it paid for the work from which those benefits are developed. In addition, the consultant is agreeing to cooperate to ensure that the client can apply for and receive the patents or copyrights. This part is needed because the consultant, having developed a process, may, under statute, actually be the only person who has the right to file such an application. Although the client owns the process, it may not have the ability to take steps to protect it. Therefore, the consultant must agree to cooperate and to do anything the client needs done to process such applications. If the parties think that the consultant will be doing work, such as developing a media or advertising campaign, that may produce trademarkable output, this clause should be amended to include "all patentable, trademarkable, or copyrightable inventions."

The following is what is generally called an indemnity clause. This clause provides that if the consultant's work under the contract results in a patent lawsuit against the client, then the consultant agrees to indemnify—that is, repay or even pay in advance—those costs and judgments so that the client is unharmed. This clause should be amended to include trademarks if the preceding paragraph also covers trademarks.

> The Consultant shall save, indemnify, and hold the Client harmless from all liability, claims, suits, judgments, damages, and losses growing out of any infringement of any patent or patent rights or copyrights covering any equipment, machine, appliance, operation, or method of operation practiced by Consultant in the performance of the Work [again, this is a defined term—what the Consultant says it will do] under the Contract.

Although the consultant is an independent contractor, the product or services delivered to the client and that the client then uses or relies on are the client's responsibility, not the consultant's. In addition to dealing with any wrongs the consultant may commit during the term of the contract, this clause also covers activities that may happen afterward. For example, if the client becomes involved in a copyright dispute about the work produced by the consultant, this broad indemnity continues to provide some degree of protection for the client if the past acts of the consultant under the contract resulted in the present copyright violation claim.

The next sample, called a general indemnification clause, is very broad. It does not deal with general torts—that is, wrongs—committed by the consultant and the consultant's employees during the retention. Although the client should not be liable for the acts of the consultant, clients and other parties are in fact sued every day for matters that are not their legal responsibility. Ultimately they may not have to pay damages, but they may incur substantial legal costs and other expenses in the preparation of the defense of such an action. This paragraph provides that the consultant will repay the client for such costs arising out of activities for which the consultant, or its agents and employees, are held legally responsible.

The Consultant shall indemnify and forever hold and save the Client harmless against any and all suits, causes of action, claims, liabilities, damages, or losses resulting from the acts or conduct of the Consultant or its agents and employees, regardless of the character of the acts or conduct and asserted by anyone whomsoever, resulting from the performance of the Work requested hereunder, and for which the Consultant or its agents and employees are legally responsible.

The next alternate paragraph limits the preceding paragraph. It limits the liability of the consultant to failure to perform in accordance with generally accepted professional standards and standards imposed by law.

The Consultant shall be liable only for any failure to perform its duties under this Agreement in accord with

(Continued)

(Continued)

[generally accepted professional standards and] the standards imposed by law. The Consultant shall have no liability under this Agreement unless such a claim is made in writing within one (1) year after the Consultant's completion of Work. The Consultant's liability to the Client for any loss or damage arising out of or in connection with this Agreement from any cause, including the Consultant's negligence, shall not exceed the total fixed monthly fees [or total compensation] received by the Consultant under this Agreement. The Client hereby releases the Consultant from any liability in excess of that amount. Under no circumstances shall the Consultant be liable to the Client for any consequential or incidental damages including, but not limited to, loss of use or loss of profit, whether or not caused by the Consultant's fault or negligence.

This kind of clause is appropriate when dealing with a consultant in what is generally regarded as a profession—namely, law, medicine, accounting, or engineering. It provides that the consultant has no liability unless there is a prompt transmission of a potential claim. In addition, it says that the consultant's liability under the contract cannot exceed its total income under the contract, to cover the special situation of the professional engaged in providing services in conjunction with a large project. For example, an architect may not be willing to provide certain consulting services in conjunction with the establishment of an industrial park if his or her liability is greater than his fee.

Insurance

The next sample paragraph is a result of the schizophrenic attitude of lawyers toward the independent contractor relationship. After lawyers have established carefully that a relationship cannot be that of an employer and employee and have advised their clients that if the clients meet all the specifications their relationship always will be regarded as that of client and independent contractor, they then advise the parties to take steps to protect themselves in case this should fail. This is one of those steps.

> The Consultant will take out and maintain all insurance required by any governmental unit to meet any statutory requirement and to protect the Consultant and the Client fully from and against any and all claims arising out of the Work performed hereunder. The Consultant will supply the Client with satisfactory evidence thereof.

Essentially, the foregoing paragraph is aimed at assuring the client that the consultant has insurance coverage, such as workers' compensation, which the employing client is responsible to obtain if the ultimate relationship between the parties is not that of independent contractor and retaining client. In a project involving large numbers of employees scattered over wide areas, such a clause is worthwhile, but not elsewhere. In a project requiring the dedication of limited numbers of personnel in an office, as distinguished from a manufacturing plant, this clause is probably redundant.

The issue remains of who pays for this coverage. Whether the client will pay the additional costs, if they are additional, should be dealt with in the contract. Fairness would seem to require that if the insurance costs are already being paid by the consultant then the client should not have to pay them. But if the consultant must take out additional policies, or increase coverage levels because of the client's requests, it would seem fair to require that those costs, incurred for the client's benefit, be paid by the client.

Applicable Law

In employment agreements, establishing which law applies is important when the employee will work in a state or country other than his or her own, if for no other reason than due to the question of the applicability of workers' compensation statutes that may apply to the consultant. In any consulting agreement with an individual, applicable law should be covered just in case the agreement is later characterized as an employment contract.

In general, stating the law applicable to a consulting agreement is important, as by its terms the contract may not specify where it is to be performed. *Usually, the place where a contract is to be performed determines which law applies.* If that is not known, the parties cannot know which law a court will apply in a dispute. It is generally accepted that an agreement stating applicable law will be respected and enforced by the courts, providing the law specified has some reasonable or foreseeable connection with the transaction at its beginning.

The following paragraph provides that the agreement is governed by the laws of a particular named state.

This Agreement shall be governed by and construed in accordance with the laws of the State of [Name].

Generally, a contract is governed by the law of the place where it is made *or* the law of the place where it is performed. Because many consulting contracts will be made and performed in the same state, a clause such as this is not *always* needed. It should be used when the consultant and client are aware that performance under the retention may occur in several states *or* the parties do not know where the consultant will be doing the work for the client. *The parties should stipulate some jurisdiction that has a reasonable relationship to the contract,* probably the state in which most of the work will be done or the state in which the corporation is located. This type of language may also be important if some or all of the work under the contract takes place outside the United States.

Amendments and Waivers
The following clause provides that the contract cannot be changed unless it is changed in writing. Even if the contract between client and consultant contains no such clause, the parties should observe this practice at all times. By placing this paragraph in the contract, the parties are actually protecting themselves against oral—that is, unwritten—changes in the agreement over which the parties may disagree.

> Any waiver, alteration, or modification of any of the provisions of this Agreement shall not be valid unless it is in writing and signed by both parties.

The next paragraph is similar, in that it also deals with the need for written documentation. It states that no waiver by either party of the default of the other waives future defaults.

> No waiver by either party of any defaults of the other party under this Agreement shall operate as a waiver of any future default, whether of a like or different character.

Such a paragraph is designed to deal with the legal doctrine on waivers, which states that if one party allows the other to deviate from the contract without either changing the contract or objecting to the deviation, then this establishes a change in the practice between the parties. The doctrine effectively allows the party that has once deviated from the contract to continue to do so without risking being found in breach of contract in any lawsuit. Now, realistically, such a series of events is unlikely, except in the most complex retentions with very far reaching forms of agreement.

Integration and Severability

The following paragraph contains what lawyers call the "integration clause." This clause is directly related to the concept that the contract should be in writing; it says that the document being signed by both parties contains the entire agreement between the parties. This wipes out any discussions that predate the contract that are not put in writing. Simply put, if something the parties talked about is not in the contract, then what they discussed is not binding on either party.

This document contains the entire Agreement between [the Client] and the Consultant. Any agreement or representation respecting the duties of either [the Client] or the Consultant not expressly set forth in this document is null and void.

A similar clause provides that if any portion of the contract is held invalid, then the entire contract will not be held invalid. This language is designed to deal with complex clauses covering liquidated damages, indemnification, and noncompetition, which are the subject of court challenges from time to time.

As drafted, the contract should reflect the actual agreement of the parties, so that it does not constitute a one-sided document. However, the legal doctrines surrounding contracts may change. Therefore, if there is a lawsuit and a court finds that one clause of an entire agreement is unenforceable, the balance of it should stand. Without a clause such as the one that follows in an extremely long, complex agreement, the courts in a contract dispute are forced to review the entire contract *and then* decide whether the clause under dispute is essential to the entire agreement. If the court finds that the problem clause is essential or critical, and that the clause is invalid for some reason, the courts will then have to declare the entire contract null and void.

> If any term or provision of this Agreement shall, to any extent, be invalid or unenforceable, the remainder of this Agreement shall not be affected and each term and provision of this Agreement shall be valid and be enforced to the fullest extent permitted by law.
>
> If the application of any term or provision of this Agreement to any person or circumstance shall, to any extent, be invalid or unenforceable, the remainder of this Agreement, or the application of such term or provision to persons or circumstances other than those as to which it is held invalid or unenforceable, shall not be affected and each term and provision of this Agreement shall be valid and be enforced to the fullest extent permitted by law.

PURCHASE ORDERS

Many businesses use purchase orders (POs) to track and control outside contracts of all sorts. Ideally, a PO is a document sent to a contractor or supplier. By agreeing to the terms in the PO, particularly on delivery, quality, and payment, an outside vendor is able to take orders from the company issuing the PO. As long as it follows the terms of the PO, it can expect full and prompt payment. Historically, POs have been used for the preapproval of the purchase of standardized goods, and to a lesser degree, relatively standardized services.

Over time, the use of the PO has been broadened. One result is that the "standard" terms in a PO expand and continue to do so. A PO that was fine for arranging for the delivery of apples for applesauce is not adequate to cover hiring a consulting engineer to design a factory. Diligent purchasing offices add, and continue to add, terms to POs to cover all possible situations.

A problem arises when POs are used not to set the terms of standardized contracts with vendors of relatively interchangeable products and services (supplies for laser copiers and repair services for printers, for example) but rather for other purposes. Such additional purposes include to manage cash flow, to control corporate employees by limiting their ability to bind the corporation to contracts of a certain size, to ensure that a division or unit stays within the budget limits set by senior management, or to enforce budget changes imposed after the approval of an annual budget.

In such situations, POs often follow, and do not precede, the contracting and contract qualification process. When that happens, very real problems arise. Typically, these have to do with two areas: payment terms and insurance.

- For example, a proposal made to a client, and accepted, may provide for an initial payment, monthly billing, and payments on 10 days net. If such a proposal has been accepted, and the consultant is then faced with a PO that provides, for example, that the client does not make prepayments, that there are no progress payments, and that the company pays on 60 days net, the opportunity for a major problem arises. Essentially, the proposal included within it a certain cash flow, which probably had an impact on price. Yet the PO issued after the proposal was submitted undercuts that flow.

- Another example lies in required insurance coverages. As POs are designed to cover more and more, they tend to include very detailed insurance requirements to be met by the company receiving them. Such requirements typically are derived from the need of a company to protect itself in construction contracts. But when applied to services consulting relationships, they usually serve only to mess things up. POs requiring proof of insurance that is not available to consultants are not uncommon. And yet, purchasing offices will withhold approval of paying an invoice if such requirements have not been satisfied.

What is the solution? If a client intends to use a PO for a consulting relationship, and the PO covers anything that the consultant (as opposed to the client contact) must do, a wise client will send a copy of the PO and all terms to any consultant with which it intends to do business. That way, the consultant will be aware of the requirements imposed by others and the client can prepare and price a proposal, taking all of this into account. While it is uncertain whether a PO, issued after a proposal has been accepted and work has begun, can change the terms of the relationship, it is certain that such practices will almost certainly affect the consulting relationship.

What happens when a consultant is faced, after it has priced and scheduled a proposed retention, with a purchase order? The following reflects efforts by consultants to protect themselves from such surprises.

Additional Terms—Client Purchase Orders. The price, due date, amount of any prepayment, payment terms, and deliverables in this Proposal are interdependent. If

(Continued)

(Continued)

the Client accepts this Proposal, whether orally or in writing, and thereafter issues a purchase order that seeks to modify the price, due date, prepayment required, payment terms, or deliverables, the Client specifically agrees that such terms will not apply to this Assignment without the specific written consent of the Consultant. The Consultant reserves the right to modify any or all of these items to reflect any changes in the project retainer required or in payment terms sought to be imposed by such a purchase order.

HANDLING PROPOSALS

Consultants are, unfortunately and correctly, very concerned that the work they do in developing a proposal for a potential client will be wasted. By this they do not mean that the client will not give them a contract—that is one of the contingencies faced in the consulting business. Rather, they are concerned that their work will be used for some other purpose. There are at least three that consistently and persistently occur:

- First, the potential client elicits one or more proposals for a given task but lacks the authority to go forward. In such cases, the proposal is being used as an internal sales device and is being sought without the knowledge of those who could really authorize it. The party that elicited the proposal takes it and tries to convince the necessary parties of the need for the work. These may be superiors, who have the actual contracting authority, or those who, in the eyes of the contact, *need* to have the work done. It is the experience of the consulting community that this use of a proposal is most often doomed to failure. But it also exploits the consultant, who was not made aware of the circumstances.

- Second, the proposal is used to develop an RFP. That is, the client essentially uses the consultant's time without paying for it. If the client wishes to have a consultant develop a complex RFP, then it should properly pay for that service.
- Third, the client shares the proposal with other consultants who are competing for the same retention. Even if the pricing is not shared, this is a very unfair practice. It gives a definite and unfair advantage to those firms that do not have to expend the time and money to develop their own proposal. They can merely exploit the work of another firm.

The following clause represents an effort by the consulting community to address all but the first point. The first can be handled only on the basis of trust. That is, the potential client tells the consultant, at the beginning, how it intends to use the proposal. This gives the consultant the opportunity to agree to that use or to decline and avoid the significant commitment of time and money.

This proposal is submitted on the strict condition that its contents will be disclosed only to you and your firm, but not to any other persons or organizations, including, but not limited to, other organizations asked to submit bids or proposals in connection with the subject of this Assignment.

A clause such as the following is used by consultants in their proposals to cover the situation wherein the client may be taking too much time to approve a proposal. For example, a client may ask for a proposal to complete a retention by May 1. On March 15, the consultant presents its proposal, which the consultant prices for completion in about one month. If the client accepts *after* April 1, then the consultant will find its performance impaired, its pricing affected, or both. By stating that it will take the Consultant a specific number of business days, the consultant covers this contingency.

Due Date: The Consultant will deliver the Assignment within [number] business days from the Client's acceptance of this Proposal. [Acceptance is effective as of the receipt of the Project Retainer specified below.]

You should note that the date is couched in terms of "business days," not days. This is an increasingly frequent term in proposals, as consultants work to schedule everything from personnel and travel to express deliveries based on the availability of others who are providing them with services. As a client, you may want to specify a date in your acceptance or have the consultant provide one in its confirmation so that both sides agree on that at the beginning.

An additional issue occurs when the consultant does not want a proposal to "hang out" for too long. The consultant handles this by providing a "trigger date." That is, the proposal says that it is valid only until a set date. This means that if the client has not decided by that date, it must come back to the consultant and ask for an extension. Then the consultant can decide if it wishes to grant the extension, withdraw the proposal, or otherwise modify it. While a client may not understand the need for this flexibility, consultants fully appreciate it. A firm such as CMV & Associates can handle only so many retentions at the same time. While it may have been ready, willing, and able to service the potential client when it first offered the proposal, after the trigger date, CMV & Associates may find that its work schedule will not permit it to offer the same time of performance or even to do the project at all.

Therefore, as a potential client, *you should never assume that the consultant will grant an extension on its proposal.* While most of the time it will, remember, when you need an extension may be the time when the consultant cannot grant it. So a client, when faced with a trigger date, should either make sure that it can respond within the time frame or ask for a more realistic one. If it needs an extension, it should get the consultant's consent in writing, some way. Even initials on a faxed extension request are much better than an okay over the telephone that can be forgotten.

The requirement that the beginning of time for the consultant to perform be tied to receiving an initial payment will be seen, particularly in proposals that:

- Are expected to cover a long time;
- May entail significant up-front costs to the consultant; and
- Are presented to clients with extremely long (i.e., from 30- to 90-day) payment terms.

Such a requirement also is used with new clients by consultants seeking, frankly, to make sure that the retention is approved and that they will be paid. Project retainers can range from 10 to 60 percent of the anticipated fees.

> Project Retainer. Any Assignment will be undertaken only (a) after receipt of a Project Retainer of at least [number]% of the midpoint of the estimated total of fees [and disbursements] or (b) in the case of established clients, after receipt of an appropriate purchase order.

WHEN IS AN ELABORATE CONTRACT NEEDED?

For most consulting relationships, a simple agreement covering key terms, including description of services, price, deliverables, due dates and payment terms, is enough. However, if the consulting relationship will continue over a long period of time, involve substantial amounts of money, or involve matters of extreme confidentiality or critical importance to the client, a more elaborate agreement should be prepared. The difference between these two contracts is not a matter of extremes; it is one of degree. A client could, of course, simply add clauses to a simple agreement to cover unique issues, such as software copyrights, without having to draft an extremely long and complex document.

NOTES

1. Kathy M. Ripkin and Leonard R. Sayles, *Insider Strategies for Outsourcing Information Systems* (New York: Oxford University Press, 1999), 25.

2. In a related matter, the client also may wish to discuss indemnification by the consultant for any patent and/or copyright infringements resulting from the retention.

5

WHAT ARE YOUR CONSULTING NEEDS?

WHICH OF THE 10 RULES APPLY

From the Top 10 Ways to Make Sure You Do NOT Get Value from Your Consulting Relationships (The More You Do, the Less Value You Can Be Sure You Will Get):

- Always make sure the decision about who to hire and what they are doing is made for someone else and on their, not your, budget.
- Don't worry about defining what are to be the deliverables or how to measure them.

MANAGEMENT'S PERSPECTIVE

From the point of view of management, there are several variables to understand and to acknowledge in the creation of a relationship with a consultant:

- To even consider retaining a consultant of any kind, someone in management must have come to a conclusion that (a) there is a problem and (b) some outside resources are needed to solve it. A major conflict arises when the person or people coming to those conclusions are not the same person or people who will be helped. The danger in such cases is that the consultant will find it difficult to work on a par with its clients, because its direct clients may not agree with *either* conclusion.

- Once managers have made the decision to look outside, the tendency is to "get ahead with it"—that is, to get someone on board and get them started. In their rush, the danger is that managers will not attempt, or will be unable or unwilling, to carefully define the problem the company faces, what they expect to be done about it, what they expect a consultant can do (and not do), and how much effort (time and money) will be involved on both sides.

" 'I was satisfied with my time [as a consultant],' says one erstwhile consultant. 'But I think the strategy [work] is a bunch of hocus pocus. If I knew my CEO had to call in [a consulting company] to tell them what product to sell, I would be irate. I would fire him. Basically, the reports we produced were these thick tomes that were basically good for keeping on top of your toilet. It's cover-your-ass stuff to present to the board of directors. They can say: "Even the [consultants] didn't know what to do.' "[1]

THE CONSULTANT'S PERSPECTIVE

For a consultant who has the opportunity to be considered for a retention, the pressure can be to get the retention no matter what. That means that the consultant, if it comes to the client early enough, may try to develop the retention so that the consultant is clearly very qualified to do the work.

Even if the retention does not appear to be significant in terms of profit, the consultant may still be interested, in that once it is in a relationship with the client, it can seek additional retentions.

DO YOU REALLY NEED A CONSULTANT?

Pressures on the client can tend to force it to enter into a consulting relationship without having thought through its other options and without having a sense of what the task is that it is seeking to have done. There is pressure, too, on a client to authorize a retention with the implicit understanding that it, the consultant, will have to redefine the work needed as the retention proceeds. The client should, before proceeding, answer the question "Do I really need a consultant?"

Inside versus Outside Consulting Service Providers

One thing to remember is that a consultant must remain independent of you and your enterprise.[2] That is so for several reasons:

- As indicated earlier, the income tax rules can convert a consultant or contractor into an employee with significant cost to you. And that conversion can be triggered by your exercise of too much control over the way in which the consultant performs services for you.
- You retain a consultant for its perspective, independence, and experience. By seeking to impose your point of view on the consultant, you effectively

93

undermine, if not destroy, the real benefit of the relationship.

That is not to say that a consultant should not be loyal to you, at least during the term of the relationship. You may want to support that sense of loyalty and involvement by including consultants in appropriate staff meetings and conference calls and copying them on internal e-mail messages. Other options include sending regular e-mail messages or memos to your consultants to keep them current on company goings-on and to emphasize how important their role is in overall company processes. You may even want to include them in some company social events.

Now that you understand how you will have to relate to the consultant, are you willing and able to hire an outside consultant to help you? Are you willing to share internal information, even with the protection of confidentiality and other clauses (see Chapter 10)? Does the fact that after a retention, the consultant may be working for a direct competitor trouble you? If so, you should consider looking within your own enterprise for consulting assistance.

While inside assistance can neither be as independent nor as much on the cutting edge as that of the leading consultants, your own staff, located elsewhere in your enterprise, may have the needed expertise, available to you, at a lower cost, and without your having to be concerned about bringing in "outsiders."

What Are the "Costs" of Outside Services?

When thinking about using outside services, that is, consultants, you should also consider what will be the costs of using them. By this we do not mean only the dollar costs, but the noncash costs as well. In evaluating the true costs of outside consulting services, you must take into account several critical factors present in virtually all consulting retentions:

- Consulting services are intangible, and they rarely involve a final product.
- Consulting services cannot be turned on and off like a faucet without additional costs to the client, to the consultant, or to both.
- Consulting services are driven by what the client thinks it needs and when it thinks that it needs the assistance, results, or report.

This means that the better you can define your problem *and* what help you need, the better you will be able to control the overall cost. The corollary is that you must be frank with a consultant about the types of services needed, the time frame of the project, your overall budget, and the nature of your expectations from the retention. *If you try to go in "cheap," you will often find that you have cost your company money, not saved it.*

But there are more hidden costs to the consulting relationship. Retaining a consultant means you are buying something before you or the consultant knows exactly what the result will be, and in some cases, whether you can get those results. In addition, if you are not satisfied with the results, the consultant cannot "repossess" them to recover its costs. Once a consulting retention has been completed and the results provided to a client, the process is out of the consultant's control forever.

Here are some tips that will help you control the economic and noneconomic costs of a consulting relationship:

- Determine what you can afford to spend for the assistance you think you need. Then try to calculate what the absence of that assistance could cost your firm, as well as what its presence could mean in terms of profits and other benefits. Then and only then you can do a cost-benefit and cost–risk of loss analysis to see if your expectations are realistic.
- Target what you would like if you could get or have done everything you want. Consultants call this a

95

"Christmas List" or "Wish List." From there, establish what will be "enough" for you to be able to improve your situation. If you later find that your ideal is unattainable or too expensive, you can shift to the fallback position without any delay.

- Consider breaking a retention into rounds or tiers. That is, when you have seen and digested the results of the first piece or tier of retention, you may be able to focus more accurately on what you need, and do not need, in the second round or tier, and so on.
- Arrange to keep in close touch with your consultant from the very beginning. If the project is important enough to pay a consultant to work on it, it is important enough for you to monitor closely.
- Establish what you already have done—how much data is already on hand, for example, that the consultant can access and use. Not only will you save money and time, but you will also provide the consultant with additional insight into what you need and do not need.

"Any information you can provide the consultant is information you don't have to pay him or her to find."[3]

- Consider retaining a consultant as a guide and teacher. In that role, the consultant can draw on its particular expertise, while you and your personnel do most of the work. The benefit here is not only a reduced economic cost but a potential transfer of skills from the consultant to you, the client.
- Get a written proposal with a fee quotation even if it covers a wide range. In general, try to avoid a proposal or quotation given in terms of dollars per hour plus costs. In those cases, you have little control, if any, over the final total cost of the retention. If that

type of pricing is unavoidable, work with the consultant to establish formal and informal controls over overall costs. These include requiring regular billings, requiring your approval for disbursements over a certain level, and having the consultant call you before the total fees and costs exceed a predetermined level.
- Consider sharing the costs of a consulting retention with other units in your company that can also use its services. This is a very good option if what you are trying to do or obtain may benefit several units.

Timing

Make sure that you bring consultants in when they are needed. It will ensure a better, and almost certainly a less costly, retention. Too often, management turns to consultants in an emergency, or in a perceived emergency.

> " '[Eighty percent] of the time, consultants are brought in for crisis intervention, after the toothpaste is out of the tube,' said [the] president of Jacobsen Consulting Group in Sunnyvale. 'Bringing consultants into the picture early ensures that they can guide initial decisions and planning efforts.' "[4]

One the prices paid by the client who hires a consultant in an emergency is that neither side is clear about what problem or problems need to be resolved, what the client expects from the relationship, and what the consultant expects that it can, and cannot, deliver.

Task Definition

Experience shows that a client's failure to define what it wants and expects before entering into a consulting

97

relationship will permeate and contaminate the entire retention.

> "As one of our best asked me after a particularly grueling steering committee session, 'Why am I having to apologize for the fact that a vaguely defined five-month project is late by three weeks when the guys in charge of it have such rotten planning skills that the one-hour meeting they call to discuss what happened lasts all afternoon.' "[5]

Who Should Be Involved?

When determining whether you need a consultant, first make sure that others in your organization who are affected agree on the need and see the need the same way. The definition of the problem is not a task that should be left to upper management alone. Rather, *all levels of management affected by the perceived problem should be consulted* before seeking other information. Upper management, middle management, and line employees each necessarily see problems from different perspectives and may see potential solutions that the other levels are unaware of. In fact, the very process of defining the problem may result in an internal solution.

Logically, those retaining the consultant should be those needing the assistance and any eventual solution. If at all possible, they should also have the necessary budgetary and managerial authority to select and retain a consultant. While this seems obvious, particularly in an age marked by claims of "team management," "customer-focused operations," "bottom-up management," and "empowerment," it often is not the situation. In our experience, employees are truly empowered so long as they pass the following two criteria:

98

- The individual (or team) has the authority to hire consultants for anything over which they have managerial authority; and
- The individual (or team) has the authority to authorize payment for such a retention.

A consultant maxim: True management empowerment exists *only* when an employee has the power to disburse funds in one contract equivalent to one year's salary *without other approval* from any higher level of management (as distinguished from controls over disbursements to prevent fraud and theft).

Unfortunately, many retentions accepted by consultants from managers at levels below the very senior-most ranks do not pass these tests. Frankly, that real separation of authority from responsibility is one reason why many consultants in a wide variety of disciplines will tell potential clients that they "work only for the CEO [COO, CIO, CFO, etc.]." It is not just a matter of the nature of their work or of their desire to be superior, in some sense, to their competitors. It also reflects an understandable desire not to get caught in the corporate tangle that often results from the following situations:

- The desire for assistance is expressed by someone who lacks authority to commit the corporation.
- The person with authority to commit the corporation needs to be "sold" on the concept or even the need.
- The one seeking assistance will not (or cannot) provide the consultant with access to the next level of management (up or down).
- A person with authority to commit the business is remote from the problem, and thus is more likely to

select a consultant based on how the consultant relates to him or her than on the consultant's ability to solve someone else's problem.

Those firms and individuals who do not restrict their consulting practice in that way are involved in a constant struggle to try to deal with "decisionmakers" when presenting information on credentials and pitching potential retentions to those who understand the need and can effectively evaluate potential consultants.

Drilling Down

As you review the problem as it has first been defined, the next question to address is whether you are facing an issue of strategy or of tactics. That is, is the question basically "Should we?" or is it "How?" Some clients will not seek or be receptive to outside advice on matters of strategy, preferring to hire outside assistance for tactical decisions only. Other clients feel strongly that they are capable of generating a tactical or operational decision but need skilled advice as to an overall strategic course to adopt. In evaluating the nature of the problem, regardless of your own culture, you should face this issue squarely.

Next, you should review the question of who can best solve the problem as now stated: outside consultants or inside employees. The benefits and reasons for employing inside consultants were mentioned briefly earlier. There are other issues pertaining to your company's operations that may affect the decision to use current employees or an outside consultant.

"Consultants often seem to be on a stretched rubber band with their

(Continued)

(Continued)

clients. If the consulting firm reports good news, it receives further assignments. If it's bad news, the rubber band is released and the consulting firm is catapulted far, far away. While it is tempting to view this trend as client misbehavior stemming from an emotional reaction to bad news, the cause is a basic lack of communications stemming from both sides of the consulting relationship.

Employees, for example, may have a vested interest in asserting that no problem exists. On the other hand, an outside consultant may have a bias toward solving the problem in the one particular way it has solved similar problems in the past. From another perspective, the decision to go outside the client may undermine employee morale if employees regard such a decision as a vote of no confidence in their ability to solve the problem or to honestly evaluate its cause. In the extreme, *some employees may see the decision to hire an outside consultant as management's conclusion that they are the cause of the problem and may think that the solution will mean their dismissal, demotion, or lack of promotion.*

In some situations, an outside consultant may be retained in order to give credibility to the obvious solution to the problem. It is often much easier to sell an unpalatable solution to senior management or a board of directors if it is proposed by an outside consultant instead of being proposed internally.

A final issue involved in the determination of whether or not to employ a consulting firm is the potential duration of the relationship between the consultant and the client. If a client is seeking advice about its activities in a new field, it must expect that it will be engaged in a long-term commitment of capital and labor. Hiring an outside consultant at the beginning may mean that the client will be making a long-term commitment to the consulting firm. On the other hand, if decisions are made internally, the client has not tied itself for the long term to a consulting firm or firms.

Once you, as the client, have decided to retain a consultant, there are several traps to avoid:

- The first is telling the consultant (directly or indirectly) the solution you think you see or need. You've hired the consultant to bring expertise to bear on solving your problem. *If you make clear what you think the solution should be, you may well expect the consultant either to decline the assignment or to come up with the solution you want, rather than the solution you may need.*

- Another trap is to completely defer to the judgment of an expert in the field. When hiring a consultant well-known in a particular area, you must realize that the consultant is providing advice. You or your management should not abdicate your judgment-making abilities and accept, point by point, the recommendation of an outside consultant without a careful evaluation.

- A slightly different trap lies in your or your management's response to the consultant's view of your needs. There is a substantial danger that management, in the belief that it has carefully defined the problem, will not give the consultant the opportunity to redefine the problem as work progresses. The most extreme example of this is when the client limits the consultant's access to individuals or operations within the client organization in the sincere belief that the consultant doesn't need certain information. The consultant can then work only with the information it receives. Screening the consultant from potentially important contacts will diminish the value of its ultimate product.

"It is no secret that management consultants are sometimes called in to provide cover for executives who don't want to carry the weight of unsavory decisions."[7]

Are all tasks appropriate for the use of outside consultants? No. Then what are inappropriate tasks? Based on the experience of consultants of all types, these are among the most common inappropriate ways in which outside consultants are being used:

- To second-guess internal decisions or personnel.
- To serve as a corporate referee among competing factions or points of view.
- To validate a decision that has already been made or is in the process of being made.
- To carry out a task for which there is no internal enthusiasm or champion.

The process of selecting a consultant requires openness. By being frank with the consultant about pitfalls, hidden agendas, and possible resources, you will save yourself money in the long run.

Are You Buying or Are They Selling?

The client that has not made a significant effort to define its needs is a prime candidate for the consultant selling a solution, and merely looking for someone with a problem who will pay.

"Before we even got the business . . . we'd always want to build the client's

(Continued)

(Continued)

problem in our own image to the extent we could.... Problem defining is really where all the action is. There was always a huge opportunity for us to spin the business our way."[8]

If the client honestly cannot define the nature of the problem or lacks the specialized resources to make an accurate assessment of its needs, such as in complex technological areas, it can retain a consultant to evaluate the nature of the problem and recommend the kind of specialist, or specialists, necessary to solve it. The result of this retention may be the preparation of what is known as a Request for Proposal (RFP).

The RFP is a device often used by governments and one that is, quite frankly, not popular with consultants. An RFP normally asks potential bidders to evaluate a problem as it is stated for them and then indicate how they would solve it, what methodology they would use, how much time it would take, and what the approximate cost would be. The reason consultants dislike this system is that in the competitive bidding common to RFPs, the consultants are investing time, effort, and money with no guarantee of receiving a contract. From the client's point of view, however, it may be a way to better define the problem and to make more efficient use of limited resources when retaining and selecting appropriate consultants.

So if you need help in determining your own needs, there is nothing wrong with using an outside consultant to help you. However, you should hire the consultant to do this and not try to clandestinely elicit help from consultants competing for your business (see below).

CONSULTANTS AND PROJECT DEFINITIONS

Consultants are, unfortunately and correctly, very concerned that the work they do in developing a proposal for a potential client will be wasted. By this they do not mean that the client will not give them a contract—that is one of the contingencies faced in the consulting business. Rather, they are concerned that their work will be used for some other purpose. There are at least three that consistently and persistently occur:

- First, the potential client elicits one or more proposals for a given task but lacks the authority to go forward. In such cases, the proposal is really being used as an internal sales device and may even be sought without the knowledge of those who could really authorize it. The party that elicited the proposal takes it and tries to convince the necessary parties of the need for the work. These may be superiors, who have the actual contracting authority, or those who, in the eyes of the contact, *need* to have the work done. It is the experience of the consulting community that this use of a proposal is most often doomed to failure. It also exploits the consultant, who was not made aware of the circumstances.
- Second, the proposal is then used by the potential client to develop an RFP, which is sent out to a number of competing firms. That is, the client essentially uses the consultant's time without paying for it. If the client wishes to have a consultant develop a complex RFP, then it should properly pay for that kind of service.
- Third, the client shares the proposal with other consultants who are competing for the same retention. Even if the pricing is not shared, this is a very unfair practice. It gives a definite and unfair advantage to those firms that do not have to expend the time and money to develop their own proposal. They can merely exploit the work of another firm.

The first of these situations can be handled only on the basis of trust. That is, the potential client tells the consultant, at the beginning, of the intended use of the proposal. This gives the consultant the opportunity to agree to that use or to decline and avoid the significant commitment of time and money. The following clause represents an effort by the consulting community to deal with all but the first point:

> This proposal is submitted on the strict condition that its contents will be disclosed only to you and your firm, but not to any other persons or organizations, including, but not limited to, other organizations asked to submit bids or proposals in connection with the subject of this Assignment.

RELATED LEGAL DRAFTING ISSUES

Once a consulting relationship has been agreed to by both client and consultant, there are still two additional contract language issues to be resolved.

Services to Be Performed

As noted earlier, one of the most common causes of trouble in the consulting relationship is the failure to define clearly the work to be performed before any work has begun. One way to counter that is for you, the client, to define what you think you need and then have the consultant refine the scope of the task through the preparation of a written proposal. That text can then be modified in negotiations and the final results incorporated into the final consulting agreement.

If appropriate, the agreement should cover such matters as regular work reports and should, if at all possible, specify the expected result or results of the consultant's performance. You may also wish to specify that you will do business only with a partner or principal of the consulting firm. Although the consultant has an implied legal obligation to do the work, diligently and in a reasonably skillful way, you are well advised to set standards of performance if there are objective ones that you can use.

The obligations of the consultant to serve and the client to pay must not be illusory ones, or the agreement will not be a valid, enforceable contract. A promise by you to employ the consultant for as long as it suits you is regarded as an illusory promise because it cannot be enforced by the consultant. In contrast, an agreement providing that the consultant will perform all services of a certain described nature that you decide need doing is not illusory.

Some businesspeople feel that imprecise contract language in a consulting agreement can be desirable because it allows room for both sides to maneuver. However, experience has shown that the dismal prospect of unenforceability as well as of future disputes over the exact scope of the work represents a major risk to the maintenance of the client-consultant relationship. In contrast, *a clear, detailed statement of the work to be performed is absolutely indispensable to creating a valid, enforceable agreement.* Any looseness in specifications should be intentional and adopted by both sides in full recognition of the business and legal risks involved.

PRECISION

Implications should be avoided; precise language should be used. For example, in an agreement where the consultant promises to provide services "as required and as the Client may direct," the consultant's duty to perform is, by implication, conditional on receiving a notice of instructions and being given a reasonable time to provide the services. If the

(Continued)

(Continued)

agreement makes no provision for the time of performance and the parties ultimately must go to court over this question, a court is then free to fix a "reasonable" time for performance. If the agreement defines the time even incompletely or imperfectly, however, a court will not be so free to attach its own notion of what is a reasonable time for performance; it will be limited by the agreement. The agreement therefore should define the time of performance if it is important either to the consultant or to the client. The definition of performance should be done with great care and specificity.

Modifications

Over time the client-consultant relationship can become quite informal, especially in agreements where the duties of the consultant are already somewhat open-ended. Extreme care must be taken to put all potential modifications of the agreement, including particular instructions, in writing. Oral modifications and instructions can cause problems under the statute of frauds; they also can be inadequate when it comes to specifying the consultant's duties vital to a beneficial outcome.

NOTES

1. "Companies Fall out of Love with Consultants."
2. This raises the troubling question of whether a consultant being given an incentive payment or even an equity position for its work can ever be independent. The question is dealt with further in Chapter 6.
3. Geddes, "How to Get the Expertise You Lack."

Notes

4. Lori Kyle, "Finding a Way through Maze of 'Consultants,'" *Business Journal of San Jose,* June 30, 1997, http://www.bizjournals.com/sanjose (January 25, 2000)

5. Herbert W. Lovelace, "The Joys of Project Management," *Informationweek,* 150.

6. Eric Garland, "CI Consultants and Clients: 'You Just Don't Understand,'" *Competitive Intelligence Magazine,* 3, no. 3 (July–September 2000):

7. O'Shea and Madigan, *Dangerous Company,* 8.

8. Anonymous, "Confessions of an Ex-Consultant," 107, 110.

6

BUDGET AND FINANCIAL ISSUES

WHICH OF THE 10 RULES APPLY

From the Top 10 Ways to Make Sure You Do NOT Get Value from Your Consulting Relationships (The More You Do, the Less Value You Can Be Sure You Will Get):

- Don't ever talk about time or money.
- Get it started with a handshake. You can always do the paperwork later.

Having decided on what is needed, the next step is to price the project and then proceed, right? Wrong. There are budget issues to attend to beforehand as well as a series of issues arising out of the costs of the retention, how it is to be billed, and how and when it is to be paid for.

BUDGETING FOR CONSULTANTS

One of the most difficult, and therefore most ignored, aspects of dealing with consultant services is the issue of budgeting for them. To many, the concept of budgeting for consulting services seems an oxymoron:

- How can you plan to hire consultants to perform services when the need for them has not yet arisen?
- How can you estimate how much you will spend for consultants to provide answers to questions that have not yet been asked?

Put that way, it seems impossible to budget for consultants; but similar objections can be raised about budgeting for almost any service purchased by any business.

In developing budgets for consulting services, you should be guided by several principles derived from management experience and common sense:

- First, how much money has your business spent on consulting services in the past? If you have previously retained consultants in similar areas, this figure can at least serve as a starting point. Many businesses will be surprised to find that they do not know exactly how much money they have spent on consulting services. This is particularly true when each strategic business unit (SBU), division, or subsidiary is allowed to define, for itself, what is covered by that term. Sound management requires that a client at least determine this, for one of the first steps in trying to control or at least predict future activity is to determine its current and past scope.
- Second, you should determine which projects or initiatives that you reasonably foresee starting or expanding in the coming fiscal year. Those businesses with truly effective long-range planning systems should already be aware of major new projects

112

or initiatives under consideration, as well as those under way, that may generate more demands for consulting assistance. These initiatives may be as narrow as reviewing the make/buy decision for one part or as broad as developing a new acquisition or divestiture strategy. In any case, reference to the long-range plan can provide an additional guide to those budgeting for consulting services.

- Third, you should look at what fundamental changes are being made elsewhere in your budget when compared with previous years. For example, a business in the midst of imposing a personnel freeze almost certainly will find that freeze will exert pressure to use consultants to replace services that formerly had been provided internally. On the other hand, a client that expects to increase its head count by adding new employees may properly estimate that the future need for consulting services will drop, not rise, when compared with the period before the new hiring was accomplished.

The mere act of asking each SBU, division, or subsidiary that prepares a budget to think about this issue may bring forth some fairly surprising answers. It may provide senior management with the first clear picture of the extent of consulting services it really uses. And that, in turn, may disclose to senior management deep-felt needs that have not come to the surface through other channels.

Budgeting is also an issue with the individual retention. As we noted before, determining your needs necessarily involves an estimation of the probable costs, if for no other reason than to estimate whether the expected gains cover the expected costs. Before budgeting for the individual retention, however, managers must keep in mind two seemingly conflicting rules:

- You get only what you pay for.
- More costly is not necessarily better.

Why are they *not* in conflict? If you do not check into credentials, you will not get what you expect when you are paying for services. On the other hand, a higher price does not mean a better product or service. It may simply reflect higher internal costs at the consultant, which affect its prices.

> "There was the Big Six provider that couldn't coax a $50,000 sales-force automation program to run on the client's laptops. After several frustrating months of waiting while the consultants miserably struggled to improve performance, [the client] scrapped the contract. It returned to ... the low-cost, contact-management program it had relied on for years."[1]

Policy Statement on Budgets

The following language could be used either in a policy on consultants or in a separate budget manual.

> Each [Unit], in its annual budget, must include a detailed description of the nature and projected cost of any consulting work being requested as well as the names of the consultants being considered.

This language, which requires a *detailed* description of projected consulting to be in the budget as well as the names of consultants under consideration, is designed to control nonapproved consulting, particularly when used with the following:

> Any outside consulting service needed after the annual budget
>
> *(Continued)*

114

(Continued)

has been approved, but that is not detailed in that budget, must be approved by [name/position] if the estimated annual cost of the consulting contract will exceed $[amount], for both fees and costs.

While the foregoing policies, when combined, produce a very rigid process for getting consulting services on an as-needed basis, they allow client management to control the excessive use of consultants, and in particular, they allow client management to steer managers to use internal consultants, if they are available.

Who Should Estimate Total Costs?

Before you even begin to talk with a consultant or consultants, you should have some idea of the cost you face in the potential retention. Obviously, as discussions or negotiations begin, or you begin to review RFPs or RFQs, you must be flexible enough to change that estimate. But, as noted earlier, the savvy client should also have a minimum version of any potential retention to which it can turn if the potential prices begin to soar beyond its envisioned budget.

In some situations a client would do well to hire a consultant to develop a potential budget. In most cases, these would be exactly the same situations in which good management could call for a consultant to develop an RFP or even an RFQ for a client. In so doing, the consultant, who of course should not be permitted to bid on this assignment, should develop an estimate of the total cost of the project, separating out fees (consultant time) from probable costs.

Should You Tell a Consultant Your Budget Limits?

While the first instinct of any client manager would be to answer, "no," that is not always appropriate. You should share some information on budget limits (such as "the total budget for this project will not exceed $100,000") in several cases:

- When you are hiring a consultant to develop an RFP or RFQ.
- When you have already worked out likely financial ranges for the desired work and are reasonably certain that quotations and proposals will not exceed that figure.
- When you believe that there are several ways in which the assignment can be done and wish to signal that you do not want to buy the gold-plated one. For example, you can be signaling consultants that you are willing to trade money for time.
- When you have asked for proposals without any price or cost data. You should at least let the consultant proposing know the range of fees and costs involved. Otherwise, after you have selected only one or two with whom to negotiate fees or from whom to solicit quotations on the final form of the assignment, you may find that they cannot provide services within your undisclosed expectations.

But, managers might ask, won't telling a consultant the maximum result in the consultant proposing to work at that figure or "billing up" to that figure? Not really. If you are soliciting proposals from several sources, *and* you let those proposing know that this is a competitive situation, good gamesmanship calls for proposals that provide the consultant with a valued retention *and* that will come in under the total cost of its likely competitors.

If you have given a consultant a no-compete contract and have told it the maximum amount you will pay, you should not expect that the consultant will either (a) bill exactly that amount or (b) come in at half that amount. Since, you must feel comfortable with a working relationship at the beginning of the retention, you will have to trust the consultant. That does not mean, however, that the consultant should not be required to verify the hours it bills, its out-of-pocket expenses, and so on when it bills you. Such verification is a reasonable trade-off for your openness.

FEE, COST, AND TERM OPTIONS

Many factors influence compensation of the consultant:

- The client often desires predictability in total cost, which may be difficult in complex retentions.
- The consultant may want maximum flexibility to use its own resources, which can be more costly to the client.
- The terms under which the consultant is paid indirectly affect the price of the retention.
- The way that the consultant is paid has, in the minds of many, an impact on the kind or even quality of advice or services that the client may receive.
- Noncash compensation, such as equity in a business, may be less costly in the short run for the client but create management issues for it in the long run.

Consultants' Position on Payment Terms

Increasingly, consultants of all sizes, from CMV & Associates to McGonagle & Company, are sensitive to payment terms. This is because *the terms under which the consultant is paid, particularly on larger or more extended retentions, directly affect the bottom-line profitability of an entire retention.*

For example, take a retention that involves disbursements of, say, $6,000 over six months. Assume that the consultant cannot bill for these until the end of the retention and is then paid by the client on a 60-day-net basis. If the disbursements were paid out uniformly over the six months, at an interest rate of 5 percent, the consultant firm could have earned $138 on that money. This is one measure of the consultant's cost of funds, or the cost of complying with the client's payment terms. It is, in essence, an additional cost to the consultant, the loss of imputed interest.

While $138 does not seem like much, assume now that this is a smaller firm, that the expenses are for air travel, and that the consultant puts them on its credit card. If they are kept there, at credit card rates from 18 to 24 percent for the same period of time, and are repaid when the money is received from the client, the hidden out-of-pocket cost to the consultant now ranges from about $500 to almost $650. If the consultant were able to bill monthly *and* the client paid on a 30-day-net basis, these indirect costs would fall dramatically.

For that reason, consultants now seek payment terms and other options to keep their project cash flow costs manageable. Such options include progress payments, seeking payment terms such as 10 rather than 90 days net, and even providing for late fees. While these terms are not always obtained, by presenting the potential client with such issues at the beginning, the consultant often has time to modify its bottom-line pricing to reflect undesirable payment procedures with its new client.

Progress Payments. All Assignments over [two weeks] in duration will entail [monthly, weekly, quarterly] progress payments. The Consultant reserves the right to suspend work if progress payments are not kept current.

> Payment Terms. The Consultant's terms for progress and final payments are [ten (10)] days net.

> Late Payments. Late payments are subject to a service charge of 1.5 percent per month on the balance due. If collection is required, the Client agrees to pay all costs of collection, including reasonable attorney's fees, filing fees, and court costs.

Most consultants do not really expect to collect the late fees as asked for in the sample, but they often do bill them to a client. The purpose is to force the client's accounting and finance personnel to handle the invoices so as to avoid embarrassment. The consultants are counting on the fact that no financial department wants to explain why it is having to pay late charges of any type.

Fee and Cost Options

Most consultants have one or two basic fee systems they are comfortable using. These may be time based, project-size/value based, or some combination of the two. But after discussions with you, a consultant should be able to quote you either a fee, a fee range, or at least an estimate of the total costs of a retention. *If a consultant cannot at least estimate the total cost of a project under consideration, it probably reflects either the consultant's inability to focus on your problems, your inability to focus on your problems, or more likely, both.* Keep talking until you both feel comfortable with deriving a price or estimate.

When looking at a variety of estimates, is the lowest estimate always the best to take? In some circumstances, where the services are truly comparable, yes, of course it is. But more often than not, *you tend to get what you pay for when you try to force down the price of a retention.* Remember, the consultant has to make a reasonable profit, based on its costs and its time. For example, do you want to start on a project only to find that the consultant cannot complete the assignment because he or she or the consulting firm goes out of business due to cash flow problems that your payment terms have made worse?

One security consultant laid down the law on how to hire security consultants. His laws have wide application. The first three are:

"Law #1: If It Says 'One Size Fits All,' It Doesn't Fit Anyone.

Law #2: Beware Of The Bargain.

Law #3: Fast, Cheap, Good—You Can Choose Two."[2]

Specific Fee Options

Over time, clients and consultants have developed a wide variety of fee plans and options. For each one, you as the client should consider the following issues, in addition to the price, or price range, you are being quoted:

- Who assumes what risk?
- What controls do you need?
- When is each type of fee arrangement best utilized?

Hourly or Other Time Charges

Under this option the consultant bills the client for the person-hours actually utilized within an agreed-on scope of work and usually at an agreed-on rate for person or level. This still requires an estimate of the amount of effort for each level of consultant involved for the consultant to staff the retention properly. This fee option tends to be the most desired by consultants, since under it they do not need to be as precise about the ultimate costs of the retention and can expect to cover their personnel, overhead, and other costs, while contributing to a profit as well.

> "Management consultants love teams."[3]

The risk here is fairly evenly divided if the consultant at least advises the client of a likely ceiling. Absent that, the client bears the risk that the retention can quickly get out of control. The best way to handle a retention based on time charges is to set a ceiling, either formal or informal. If that is impossible, then the agreement should require that the consultant provide billing on a monthly basis, that the consultant advise the client of its estimated charges for the next month, and perhaps that the client should be advised when time charges, even if unbilled, hit a designated level.

Fixed Fees
Fixed fees are best used when both sides have a clear vision of the task involved, and where the deliverables can be clearly, and objectively, measured at the end of the task. That, of course, requires hard work on both sides of the retention. Because of that, some consultants are reluctant to use this fee structure, since they take the risk that the estimate of the time they need to devote to the project is too low. Experience shows that the estimates are rarely too high, particularly when a fixed price is sought in a competitive bid or proposal situation.

The firms with the very largest overhead, such as McGonagle & Company, have tried, over time, to avoid such arrangements as a matter of policy. However, do not assume that this is a manner of pricing that can be used only with smaller firms; even units within firms such as KPMG undertake contracts like this.[4]

The client benefiting from such an arrangement should still monitor work, in particular the level and quality of personnel devoted to the retention. A shift to less experienced, and therefore less costly, personnel in the latter stages of the retention may be a warning sign that the consultant has mispriced its proposal and is trying to cut its own costs.

A situation where the consultant offers a fixed price but also sets a fixed (that is, a maximum) number of hours of work is really just a variation of an hourly-rate fee structure.

Bracketed or Ranged Fees

This option is a variation of fixed fees; here the consultant provides a range within which the retention will fall. This is, as are most estimates, usually based on hourly or other time charges plus indirect expenses and profit. By giving a range, the consultant tends to minimize the risk that it is underpricing the retention. However, the client should be sure that the consultant is not using the range as an indirect way to buy into a retention. That is, the lower range is used to attract the client's interest, while the higher end of the range is where the consultant really expects the retention to be billed.

Unless the client asks for progress estimates—that is, a statement at the midpoint of the retention or later of where the range of billings is expected to fall—the client is at the mercy of the consultant's determination of the final bill.

Bracketed or ranged fees, however, can be very useful when the nature of the retention is such that the effort of the consultant may vary due to client demands. For example, if the client is unsure if it wants a final presentation to senior management in addition to a final report, the consultant should factor in the possibility of the additional work (and travel) to figure the upper end of the range.

Contingent Fees

Contingent fees are those where the amount, or even the payment of the fee, is based on some factor other than the completion of the retention. These can vary widely. Examples of contingent fees include payment if a reorganized subsidiary is sold, if a private company goes public, and so on. Such fee arrangements are also known among consultants as "on spec work." That is slang for "work being done on a speculative basis." While contingent fees are similar to percentage and other fee arrangements (discussed shortly), they differ in one key aspect. The payment of a contingent fee depends on the triggering event. For the other fees, it is the amount of the fee that varies depending on the outcome.

Under this arrangement, the consultant bears the risk that the fee will not be paid. Of course, if the client has agreed to pay all direct costs, the consultant's risk is reduced but not eliminated. If the contract provides that the repayment of costs is contingent as well, then the consultant bears a huge risk.

For that reason, such contracts are very unpopular with consultants. They should be of concern to clients as well because of their effect on the independence of the consultant's work or advice. As the consultant has a direct financial interest in the occurrence of the triggering event, rather than in giving the client the best effort possible, the consultant can find itself in a very different relationship. No longer is it an independent provider of objective assistance. Now it has a real interest in a certain outcome. In some cases, this can even drive the consultant to seek the equivalent of a management or comanagement position in the client's business to ensure the happening of the event on which it will be paid.

"The proposed rule reiterates that an accountant cannot provide any ser-

(Continued)

(Continued)

vice to an audit client that involves a contingent fee. Contingent fees result in the auditor having a mutual interest with the audit client in the outcome of the work performed."[5]

Percentage Fees

Percentage fees are a fee arrangement where the payment to the consultant is usually a percentage of the cost of the total project being managed or supervised. This arrangement is most often found in construction projects and similar situations. The total cost is used as a surrogate to measure the total effort required of the consultant for supervising the total project. A major concern here is the lack of incentive for the consultant to try to save money on the total project. Therefore, if such a fee is used, the client should protect its interests by setting a ceiling on the compensation paid, requiring regular reporting of changes in subcontract work or in the amounts expected to be spent, and so on. Another option is to pay the consultant a fixed fee plus a smaller percentage of the project price.

The term is also used when a consultant's compensation is, in part or in whole, a percentage of the total costs saved as a result of a particular project. In such cases, the arrangement can be an incentive to cut too deeply in order to generate a greater fee by seeming to cut total costs. In that case it can yield a hidden trade-off of short-term gains for long-term damages and possibly even losses. Of course, the consultant is taking the risk that the client will not implement all of the changes it recommends. As can be seen, then, it can put the consultant in the situation of trying to force the client to do what it recommends, or even of trying to assume a management position to ensure that the changes are carried through.

An additional issue in these contracts is measurement. What is the base from which savings are to be measured,

124

how are they to be measured, and over what time frame? If percentage (saving) fees are to be used, these issues should be carefully documented before any work is started.

Value-of-the-Assignment Fees

Value-of-the-assignment fees are also called gain-sharing relationships or value-based pricing. They are similar to percentage fees except that they typically involve the consultant having some or all of the fee based on a positive outcome at the end of the retention, such as an increase in sales, profits, and the like. However, just as with percentage fees, these require a very clear definition of how to measure the gain. Both sides must agree at the outset what constitutes a successful outcome and should clearly delineate each side's responsibilities.

Should your consultant be paid on the basis of "success"? What about getting a piece of the pie? Consider the comments of the U.S. Securities and Exchange Commission as it struggled with the question of how to keep auditors independent, and appearing so:

> Independence will be impaired if the accountant...has a direct or material indirect business relationship with the audit client, other than providing professional services or acting as a consumer in the ordinary course of business.... When the accountant acts, temporarily or permanently, as a director, officer or employee of an audit client, or an affiliate of the audit client, or performs any decision making, supervisory, or ongoing monitoring functions, the accountant becomes part of the very entity he or she is auditing.[6]

As with percentage fees, there is the issue of the client implementing a consultant's recommendations. Some consultants have tried to obtain from the client a precommitment to undertake all of its recommendations. While this is an effort by the consultant to try to ensure payment of its fee, it does place the client in a subservient position. It is less than desirable in many contexts as it tends to put the consultant too close to the client's business.

Even if the parties can resolve measurement and implementation issues, they should, at the creation of the agreement, also agree on a way of dealing with exogenous factors, such as sudden changes in oil prices, which can quickly change the effective level of the gain (either up or down).

Retainer Fees

Retainer fees are paid whether or not the consultant is used by the client. They are used in situations where the consultant's expertise is extremely valuable to the Client but is not needed regularly. An additional factor is that the consultant is usually required to keep itself available to the client. This may prevent the consultant from taking other retentions, particularly from competitors of the client. Thus the need for a payment.

Some retainer fees are designed to be used up. That is, the client is paying for up to X hours of the consultant's time over some period of time (per month, over the term of the retainer). If the client needs more time, many retainers provide a rate or rates that will be applicable to such efforts.

Because the client pays the fee even if it does not use any consultant services, the client bears the risk that it is paying for services it will never need. On the other hand, because the consultant must hold itself available for the client, it may have to decline a retention during the term of the retainer.

Equity Fees

Under this arrangement, the consultant will take an ownership or investment position in the client or in a business generated as a result of the retention as a part or even as all of the fee. This is becoming an aggressively sought-after position, particularly by the very large multinational management consulting firms. They see that such arrangements allow their personnel to share in the long-term financial gains produced by their expertise. In fact, it is this desire that some industry observers believe is driving the separation of the very large management consulting firms from their historical position in the global accounting firms.[7]

Even more than the value-of-the-assignment or similar fee situations, equity fees clearly raise the issue about the independence of the consultant with respect to the client. That is, *if the consultant takes a capital position in a client, does that affect the independent nature of their advice?* More important, does it constitute a conflict of interest with respect to any of its current clients?

As this is a relatively new approach, there is another question that has barely been raised. That is about future retentions. Can the consultant that now holds an equity investment in former client A take a retention from a direct competitor, B? If so, is it ethical for the consultant to take an equity fee from that company as well?

Other Variations

There are probably as many types of fee arrangements as there are client-consultant relationships. For example, the parties may wish to provide for a bonus/penalty fee. In that case, the consultant is paid a basic fee under one of the more traditional fee bases. But that total fee is adjusted, within agreed-on limits, to reflect the financial results of the retention. If the retention produces results above those expected (or promised), there is a bonus; if they fall short, the fee is reduced by a penalty. As with the percentage and other similar fee arrangements, there are two key concerns here:

- The need for clear definitions of what is being measured; and
- The concern that this fee arrangement undermines the independence of the consultants.

Yet another variation is deferred fees. These fees are paid only after the consultant's recommendations are implemented. But unlike the value-of-the-assignment fee, they are paid whether or not the client gains from the retention. Under this option, the consultant is taking the risk that the client will be unable to afford fees that it could not afford at the beginning of the retention.

HINTS ON CONTROLLING COSTS

Consider when and how to require the consultant to use your own facilities, including the copy center, word processing staff, travel office, and so on. Have the consultant bound by the same policies that govern the employees with whom the consultant will be working, including those on travel and entertainment expenses.

Do not allow subcontracting as an expense category.

For more on the application of corporate policies to consultants, see Chapter 3.

Contract Issues: Fees and Billing

There are many ways in which the consultant may be compensated for its services. And there are some important issues involved in billings and payment procedures.

Fees and Costs

Compensation under a consulting agreement can be an area of potential controversy, particularly when it is left at all open-ended. Where open-ended pricing is the only feasible approach, the consultant can be required to let the client know when a predetermined threshold figure is imminent so that the client can take steps to control its total financial exposure.

On the other hand, if the contract pays costs plus a fixed fee, there should be a defined maximum on the total costs. Further, if the agreement permits the consultant to pass on increases in its own personnel costs, the consultant should give prior notice of those new costs and the agreement should specify when such increases will be reimbursed.

When a consulting agreement provides for payment of a flat fee upon the completion of a task, both sides must consider what compensation, if any, the consultant should receive if full performance becomes impossible. If the agreement is with an individual consultant, the law appears to be that the consultant is entitled to the fair value of any services rendered for which, because illness or death prevented his or her completing performance, he or she could not recover—unless the agreement clearly makes the whole performance a prerequisite to payment for any part of the work. When outside events of other kinds, such as a supervening law or the conduct of a third person on whose cooperation the ability to perform depends, make complete performance impossible, payment should be provided to the extent of the fair value of partial performance rendered while performance was still possible.

If the consultant is to be paid a fixed fee, the contract can simply state the following:

The Consultant will be paid US$[amount] for all work performed under this Agreement.

The following paragraph deals with compensation and expenses by setting a total fee for all work performed, payable on satisfactory completion of the work. This enables the client to judge whether the work is, in fact, satisfactory. Of course, that decision must be made in good faith. The clause cannot be used as a way of terminating the agreement to avoid paying the consultant.

Compensation and Expenses. The Client will pay you a total fee of $[amount] for all work performed hereunder on satisfactory completion of the work. You will receive reimbursement for the actual cost of reasonable expenses arising out of the work performed under this Agreement [not to exceed $[amount], subject to the approval of the Client. You shall deliver an itemized statement to the Client on a monthly basis that shows fully the work being performed under this Agreement and all related expenses. The Client will pay you the amount of any authorized expenses within [thirty (30)] days of the receipt of the itemized statement of all expenses submitted together with receipts for all hotel, car rental, air fare, and other transportation expenses and for all other expenses of $25.00 or more.

The paragraph provides for the reimbursement of expenses but requires that the consultant submit an invoice and that the expenses be "reasonable." The client has the option of requiring that all expenses conform to an established client policy (which has previously been given to the consultant). If a consultant is to receive reimbursement for any expenses, the terms of that reimbursement should be spelled out in advance, and discussed before the consultant presents a quotation or proposal. It is quite unfair to elicit a proposal or quotation and then to inform the consultant that the expenses will be handled according to a system with which he or she is unfamiliar.

This section also provides for a statement of "the work being performed under this Agreement," which allows the client to decide whether the expenses sought are reasonable in light of what the consultant has actually done. The client is obligated to make prompt payment to the consultant. If the client wishes, the total expenses under the contract may be limited by the language shown in the brackets. If the client wishes to impose specific expense limitations, such as not permitting first-class travel, they should be specified here, or reference should be made to a written set of company expense and entertainment standards given to the consultant. If such standards exist, this agreement may read as follows:

> You will receive reimbursement for the actual cost of reasonable expenses arising out of the work performed under this agreement in accord with the written standards of the Client, attached as Exhibit X hereto and specifically made a part of this Agreement.

If the client provides certain benefits, such as trip insurance, for the consultant as a matter of course, the consultant should be informed of this and should not be permitted to bill the client for those expenses on its own. The consultant then should be given necessary beneficiary and enrollment forms to complete. Care should be taken, however, not to offer to the consultant strictly employee benefits, as the consultant is not an employee and must not be treated as one for liability and other reasons discussed earlier.

An alternative may see the consultant billing the client an amount that is to be determined. For example, the consultant might quote a fee and costs in a particular range. The client's contract could handle this in one of two ways:

> The Consultant will be paid [between $yy,yyy and $xx,xxx (US)] [no more than $xx,xxx (US)] for all work performed under this Agreement.

In more complex situations, the client and consultant may wish for payment for the consultant's time worked on the project to be made as follows:

The work performed under this Agreement will be on a billing-rate basis in accordance with the following rate structure:

Maximum Number of Days   Rate per Day
                               $

Partial days will be prorated on an hourly basis.

[Alternative:

Maximum Number of Hours   Rate per Hour
Partial hours will be billed in 10-minute increments.]

The above rates cover all direct labor. Expenses incurred, such as travel, subsistence, copying, etc., will be billed at cost.

An option that covers the situation where the consultant may use several people on the assignment is to set a fee range for each person and for the consultant to give a copy of that to the client.

Attached as Schedule A is a schedule of fees and other costs to be paid by the Client in connection with the Work to be performed by Consultant for the Client. Schedule A is incorporated by reference into this agreement.

In these situations, the parties should agree on an hourly or daily rate for the personnel, either as a group or individually, unless the parties wish to provide that the services rendered by the consultant will be billed to the client at the consultant's usual rates. Although that may be a common practice, it may not always be desirable. For example, the client may not even know what those rates are until it has received its first bill. To avoid misunderstandings, *the parties at least should be aware of the usual rates prior to the rendering of the first bill or the performance of any services.*

Another type of fee arrangement is the cost-plus contract. That is one where the consultant bills the services of its own personnel on a cost basis, which is calculated on the basis of their annual salary. The consultant will pay for other agreed-on services. The consultant is then paid a management service fee in the form of an override or percentage add-on.

The consultant may be paid on the basis of some contingency—for example, 25 percent of the amount saved the client by the consultant's activities over the term of the contract. *In every case, the parties should deal with two items: fees and costs. As a rule, the parties should leave nothing to implication.*

- If the consultant is not to be reimbursed any costs, the contract text should specify this.
- If the consultant is to receive reimbursement for only some costs, the contract should state so and define which are reimburseable and which are not.
- If the parties intend that the consultant can revise the fee schedule over the term of the agreement, to protect the client the agreement should provide that any change in the fee schedule applies to new work only, as opposed to existing or past work.

Yet another option is to pay the consultant a fixed fee and to have the client cover certain costs.

The Client will pay the Consultant for the Work performed under this contract as follows:

(a) A fixed monthly fee of $[amount] and
(b) The recoverable costs listed in Schedule B, which is attached and incorporated in this agreement.

The recoverable costs are set forth in schedule B, which is to be attached to the contract. The sample schedule B that follows is an extremely broad, far-reaching schedule of this kind. This one is designed to pay virtually all of the direct costs of the consultant for performing under this contract.

SCHEDULE B—RECOVERABLE COSTS

The Client will reimburse the Consultant for all reasonable costs and expenses incurred by Consultant in the performance of the Work. Such costs and expenses generally include, but are not limited to, the following:

1. Payroll and Related Personnel Costs. Costs and related expenses incurred by the Consultant in accord with its established personnel policies, including all salaries and wages of personnel engaged directly in the performance of the Work, plus the Client's established rate for all employee benefits and allowances for vacation, sick leave, holiday, and the company portion of employee insurance and retirement benefits, all payroll taxes, premiums for public liability and property damage liability insurance, Workers' Compensation and employer's liability insurance and all other insurance premiums measured by payroll costs, and other contributions and benefits imposed by any applicable law or regulation. This rate may be adjusted annually to reflect increased costs, as verified by the Consultant's independent auditors.

2. Overhead Expenses. Rent, leasehold improvements and expenses, office equipment, fixtures, and supplies.

(Continued)

(Continued)

3. Other Direct Costs. All other costs incurred in the performance of the Work, including such costs as:

    a) Travel, subsistence, relocation, and return of personnel engaged in the performance of the Work. [These costs shall be in accord with the Client's then current policies for its own employees.]

    b) The actual costs of all materials and supplies used in the performance of the Work.

    c) Information and communications services at cost to the Consultant.

    d) Subcontracts and other outside services and facilities, as approved by the Client, at cost to the Consultant.

    e) All taxes and assessments incurred in connection with the performance of the Work and paid by the Consultant, excepting only taxes levied directly on or measured by net income and corporate franchise taxes.

    f) Insurance and bonding costs, fees, and expenses.

This kind of broad-scale approach is most often used when the consultant is required to make a substantial dedication of employees and resources to a project for a prolonged period of time and for a fixed fee. It can also be appropriate when the parties can foresee additional or other duties that may later be added to a core set of duties. In those cases, the consultant may be forced to add additional people to its payroll to meet the client's new needs. A recoverable costs schedule does not have to be so elaborate. The client and the consultant can agree to reimburse no costs or only such limited costs as they specify.

NONASSIGNABILITY

The decision to make the consulting agreement non-assignable can be particularly important when considering costs. For example, in a cost-plus agreement, which is nonassignable, the compensation paid to any subcontractor may become a reimbursable cost, in addition to the consultant's fee, potentially increasing the total amount the client may have to pay. On the other hand, if this task is one that the consultant can assign, the client may be able to insist that the additional work be paid for from the consultant's own fees.

Billing Procedures

To get paid, a consultant has to give the client a bill. And the client may want to use the billing process as a control point. The sample clause that follows requires the consultant to deliver monthly statements. Such statements are designed to inform the client about expenses and costs to date as well as to indicate which people are currently involved in the retention. This serves to avoid running up excessive costs. It also enables the client to prepare more adequate evaluations of the consulting firm and its employees for its own future use. On the other hand, it also provides for prompt payment to the consultant of its monthly statements. This is particularly important to the consultant when it is seeking reimbursement for substantial costs and expenses.

Statements shall be delivered to the Client on a monthly basis. All statements shall show the nature of the Work performed, the individual(s) performing the task, the

(Continued)

136

(Continued)

title of such individual(s) and the days [hours] involved. Such statements shall also include, in itemized form, Consultant's recoverable costs arising out of its performance of the Work. The Client agrees to pay Consultant the amount of such statements within fifteen (15) days after receipt thereof.

If the consultant is being retained for a long period of time, particularly if the firm will be providing various services through work orders, the client may want to establish a standard billing procedure. If the client does not have billing procedures, such as those built into a purchase order that applies to the retention, it might consider adopting a billing form (see the sample that follows) for consulting assignments. You should note that this form provides that the consulting firm being retained has some standard daily or hourly rate, which will be used in this case. In addition, it clearly notes that any other persons outside the consulting company may be used on the project only after they have been retained by the client, not by the consultant. This effectively prevents the consultant from subcontracting its work to another firm that was not even considered by the client.

[The Client] is to be charged for services provided to it only on the basis of the Consultant's standard hourly or daily rate for the categories of employees performing the services [which have been provided to the Client or which are attached to this contract]. In addition, the Client will be charged for services rendered by other consultants, accountants, or experts only when they have been retained directly by [the Client].

The billing procedures can deal with billing statements and the cycle upon which they should be submitted. The following language provides that the consultant is not required to submit bills for nominal amounts, but that he or she should submit significant bills every 30 days.

To exercise special financial control in very large, long-term retentions, the consultant could be required to submit a bill every calendar quarter, even if it has not done so beforehand. An additional issue, making sure that bills are paid within the appropriate tax, or fiscal, year is covered by a sentence requiring that statements for the period at the end of the cycle, such as through November 30, must be submitted before the books close, such as by December 10. Finally, to deal with the estimated year-end obligations of the unit in question, the policy can require that the work at the end of the period, that is, December for a tax year, be estimated and submitted at the beginning of the next month, here January.

A statement for services rendered may be submitted to [the Client] as frequently as the Consultant desires. In any case, a statement must be submitted to [the Client] within 30 days following the end of any month in which the total services and disbursements exceed $[fixed amount, such as $10,000] and within 30 days following the end of each calendar quarter. For accounting purposes, a statement through November 30 must be submitted by December 10. A written estimate of the total December statement must be submitted on the first working day each January.

Billing procedures may also set forth the items the bill should cover, enabling the client to evaluate the quantity of time spent on the project as well as the level and number of employees involved. This type of process would be desirable when a retention covers a long period of time and entails the work of a number of the consultant's employees.

Each bill will show:

The number of hours [days] spent by each employee of the Consultant on the assignment(s);

The billing rate for each employee of the Consultant on the assignment;

The nature of the services performed during the billing period;

The total disbursements made to other consultants, accountants, and experts [note: if that is allowed];

All expenses and disbursements, itemized; and

The total due the Consultant for the billing period.

It is particularly important that the client's management have a general idea whether the work being done requires the participation of high-, medium-, or lower-level consultant personnel. Client management should be able to determine this from these types of billings.

Note that the billing procedures in the preceding sample also require that the consultant's statement detail the services performed during the period covered by the statement, even though it might be assumed that the client's manager in charge of the assignment is fully familiar with the nature of the services being performed by the consultant during the statement period. This detail serves several purposes:

- First, it operates as a control on the consultant to ensure that accurate records are being kept of the services being performed and for which the client is being billed. This is critical, as many of the services being performed may be off-site and without the prior specific approval of the client.
- Second, it lets the client see early on if the consulting firm is heading in a wrong direction on the project. For example, if a marketing project involves a question of retailing goods through discount stores, statements that outline meetings with wholesalers or surveys of factories might raise a question. The manager then has time to make sure that the individuals working on the project understand the limited nature of their assignment.
- Third, it enables client management to evaluate the work of the consulting organization as a whole, as well as that of its individual consultants. This can be particularly useful if a manager has to complete a consultant appraisal and review form. That is because it permits the appraisal both of an organization and of individuals, who later may be a part of another consulting organization.

NOTES

1. Deborah Asbrand, "Good Help Is Hard to Find," *LAN Times,* September 9, 1996, http://www.LANtimes.com (January 17, 2000).

2. John Nolan, "Six Laws for Choosing a Security Consultant," *Access Control and Security Systems Integration,* August 1996. reprinted at http://www.intellpros.com/SIXLAW.html (September 28, 2000).

3. Biswas and Twichell, *Management Consulting,* 31.

4. Mark Leon, "Client View: Five of a Kind," *Consulting Magazine,* February 2000, 15–17.

5. U.S. Securities and Exchange Commission, "Fact Sheet: The Commission's Proposal to Modernize the Rules Governing

the Independence of the Accounting Profession," June 27, 2000.

6. U.S. Securities and Exchange Commission, "Fact Sheet."

7. Such as in the case of Ernst & Young. See Margot Gibb-Clark, "Merged Firm Aims to Bring Best of Both Worlds," *The Globe and Mail* (Canada), June 5, 2000, M1.

7

FINDING AND SELECTING THE RIGHT CONSULTANTS

WHICH OF THE 10 RULES APPLY

From the Top 10 Ways to Make Sure You Do NOT Get Value from Your Consulting Relationships (The More You Do, the Less Value You Can Be Sure You Will Get):

- Don't ever have the final decision maker or end user involved in interviewing potential firms. (Alternate: Always make sure the decision about whom to hire and what they are doing is made for someone else and on their, not your, budget.)
- Allow someone to retain a firm for which he or she previously worked.
- Always select bigger over better. (Alternate: Pick a name other people know over one they do not.)

143

FINDING A CONSULTANT

If at all possible, before beginning a new major retention, you as the client should develop a new list of potential consultants. In some situations time may keep you from doing so, but as noted earlier, in such cases there are almost certain to be problems in ensuring a satisfactory retention in any case.

Even if you have previously done this, you should do it again. That is because a list made up only six months ago for this very task may no longer be useful:

- A key firm on your list may have lost some or all of the staff who possess the expertise you are seeking.
- New technology or management concepts may have been developed that were not available when you made up the list.
- New firms may have come into being with the expertise you need.
- Firms that previously did not make the list because of a lack of qualifications may have added staff with those very qualifications.

Internal Resources

First, if your firm has created them, refer to existing consultant evaluation reports and appraisals. Use them to identify consultants with experience with your firm. However, do not limit yourself to the firms on these lists. Ask other managers about their experience with consulting firms that appear to be qualified for your assignment. In addition, survey key employees, particularly those who will be involved with the retention, for their suggestions. Not only might they give names of firms that are more currently involved with the area, but asking them for names will help the eventual consultant by creating a better internal environment.

While asking others in your company what consultants they have used can be a good first step, it should not be the only one. *Just because an individual or firm was effective on one project does not guarantee that it is suited for another even for the same client.* And the reverse is also true: Just because an individual or firm was *not* effective on one project does not automatically mean it is not suited for another retention from the same client. Why? The past and present assignments may differ significantly in terms of skills, experience, or other critical qualifications.

External Resources

Potential consultants may be identified and located through a combination of the following resources:

- Research the trade press covering your industry, as well as the more general business press, for discussions of the activities of consultants and consulting firms working in the particular area.
- Review directories of consulting organizations for leads. Remember, mere membership is not the same as having experience or credentials. Even association credentialing programs may not be of assistance.
- Check associations for their referral services, particularly in very exotic or niche areas.
- Check for articles or books published by principals and employees of consultants. This can lead you to their firms. However, you should first read them. Do they seem to match your needs?
- Advertise, either with your company's name or blind (without your name). If you advertise blind, you will probably get fewer responses than if you used your name.
- If you are a small business owner, look for nontraditional sources, such as other business owners who may be able to help you.[1]

145

- Check out Internet resources. There is a growing, almost bewildering variety of centers, bulletin boards, services, and the like. Some charge fees; others do not.

THE INTERNET AND CONSULTANT RECRUITING

There are a growing number of Internet-based services that say they help match independent companies, including consultants, with companies seeking help. These include:

www.onvia.com
www.guru.com
www.Starbelly.com
www.jobsleuth.com

These services are designed primarily to appeal to the individual or small consulting firm. In addition, they usually focus on narrowly defined skills. Today, the issues involved in using them are as follows:

- Decide whether you want to post the project you are seeking help with or search for potential bidders yourself. In the former case, you trade control over the description of the project for the accumulation of parties who are clearly interested, whether or not they are qualified. In the latter, you tend to keep control over the project description (which is important if you have not yet gotten to that stage), while seeking to locate those whose qualifications or areas of interest appear, to you, to meet your needs. However, these individuals and firms may not be interested in this project.
- If you have a task with very unusual needs, Internet sources can be quite helpful in locating specialists in niches where you have not had existing contacts.
- These lists tend to be much more up-to-date than refer-

(Continued)

(Continued)

ence aids, such as directories, membership lists, and the like.

- If your task is very general, you risk being flooded with applicants or candidates.
- If you are not satisfied with companies you have used in the past, this can be an effective way to find replacements, or at least competitive bids.
- Where you are required to, or feel that you should, seek out the widest variety of potential contractors. Using these services should provide you with access to potential contractors well beyond the lists that your firm may retain.

In developing a list of potential consultants, avoid the trap of going only for the "old, established consulting firm." Just because a consulting firm is large and has been around a long time does not mean that it provides the services you need or that it can provide the quality of services you want on a cost-effective basis. *Never assume, or even believe, that every firm does everything equally well.* For reasons of efficiency and equity, also seek out more specialized firms. Being smaller, they may be more responsive; being newer, they may be more aggressive; being specialized, they may be more cost-effective.

Each of the resources listed above should turn up the names of individuals and organizations, but your search does not end there. A diligent manager will expand the list creatively before limiting it. Individuals identified with a consultant two years ago may now be with another firm; this new firm also may be a candidate. A large consulting firm identified with a major government contract covering issues similar to those under study by your company may have subcontracted specific portions of the contract to more specialized firms; those firms should be added to the list and the larger firm removed.

SELECTING A CONSULTANT

Security consultant John Nolan laid down the law to corporate security directors on how to hire security consultants:

"Law #5: There's No Such Thing As Instant Experience.
Law #6: Seek A Partner, Not An Accomplice."[2]

Now that you have developed a list of potential consultants, what do you do? First, make sure you have avoided these five common errors:

- Limiting the list to names you know.
- Keyholing.
- Prepricing.
- Limiting the solutions.
- Ignoring conflicts of interest.

Once you have done that, you can start narrowing down your list to a few or even one finalist.

Common Errors

Once you have a list of potential consultants to consider for a retention, avoid making a number of all-too-common errors in making your final selection.

The Known Name

"In the comfortable 'good old days,' many executives bought [computer

(Continued)

(Continued)

technology from IBM] as a risk averse strategy. If problems occurred, they couldn't be blamed for buying an off-brand or the wrong technology. Many of those same executives adopt the same strategy in outsourcing their new [information systems] work to a Big Blue equivalent, the best name brands.... [But] even the best often overstate their competencies..., misconstrue or fail to fully comprehend their client's requirements, use inexperienced personnel, and shortcut testing to meet unrealistic schedules."[3]

As suggested earlier, in developing a list of potential consultants, you should be careful to avoid the trap of the "old, established firm." For one thing, you should not assume that every firm does everything well. But there is another reason clients tend to limit the field to well-known firms rather than including lesser-known, but more qualified ones. In this case the issue is purely defensive. That is, an insecure manager subconsciously believes that he or she can deflect any criticism that may arise after the retention is over. "If the project fails and I selected CMV & Associates, then any failure will be at least partially my fault, because no one else ever heard of this firm. But if I select McGonagle & Company, and the project fails, I cannot be criticized. After all, I went with one of the biggest."

Keyholing
The term *keyholing* is taken from livestock breeding. It means that breeders severely limit their gene pool, and thus genetic diversity, by going back to a winning stud again and again. While this can help produce winning animals in the short run, in the long run it is detrimental to the overall development of the breed.

The same is true with consulting services. A client that goes back again and again to the same consulting firm (or just a few firms) for assistance may get what appears to be good assistance in the short run. But in the long run it faces the significant risk that it will have lost opportunities to be exposed to and use new approaches and concepts.

> "[Many huge companies] that first bought McKinsey's top dollar advice ...then saw McKinsey veterans shift loyalties and join executive ranks, frequently turning back to their old employer to buy consulting services."[4]

Even the client that does not do this can face keyholing of a sort. That happens when a former employee of a consultant, now working for the client, turns to his or her old firm for consulting services. Such relationships should be strongly discouraged. This is not to say that a former employer should be disqualified from competing for a retention. But the operative concept here is "competition"—that firm should have no competitive advantage because of its previous relationship with a manager or executive. It should get a retention based only on the fit of its proven credentials to the identified need. In client companies where this pattern is ingrained, management may want to set a policy that all such awards, that is, to previous employers, be on a competitive basis only.

Pricing not Selecting

> "Looking for an inexpensive fix, companies frequently pick up people between jobs who are selling themselves as consultants. They may have technical expertise but lack the broad skills necessary to operate independently of an organization or deal with a client relationship.
>
> "They may fall short of a client's performance expectations, or worse, leave before the project is completed to pursue an attractive job offer."[5]

When reviewing the list of potential consultants, you should not strike any name because you expect that the retention will be too expensive. If that is possible, you should rethink the scope of the retention rather than change the field available for assistance.

A similar situation is where client reviews a list to look only for consultants who might be expected to come in with the very lowest prices. Again, the issue is not the price but the quality of the advice. Bad advice that is inexpensive is not a bargain.

Limiting the Solution
Even when you have made the decision to hire a consultant, there are several traps to avoid:

- The first is telling the consultant (directly or indirectly) the solution you see. A consultant is hired to bring its expertise to bear on the problem. If you make clear what you think the solution should be, or even worse, must be, you may well expect the consultant either to decline the assignment or to produce the solution you want, rather than the solution you may need.
- A second trap is to completely defer to the judgment of an expert in the field. When hiring a consultant well-known in a particular area, you must realize that the consultant is providing advice. You or your management should never abdicate your judgment-making abilities and accept, point by point, the recommendation of an outside consultant without a careful evaluation.
- A slightly different trap lies in how you or your managers respond to the consultant's needs during the retention. There is a substantial danger that management, in the belief that it has carefully defined the problem, will not give the consultant the opportunity to redefine the problem as work progresses. The most extreme example of this is when the client

limits the consultant's access to individuals or operations within the client's organization in the belief that the consultant does not need certain information. The consultant can work only with the information it receives. If the consultant is screened from potentially important contacts, the value of its ultimate product will be diminished.

Conflicts of Interest

You should think about asking consultants, before considering them for a full-blown interview, whether they are currently working on other retentions that could create a conflict of interest for them. A useful standard to apply is the same standard applied to employees—that is, is the other business in a directly competitive situation? You can also address the issue in the agreement with the consultant, so that it does not happen during the retention. The forms discussed in Chapter 10 provide sample language governing corporate opportunities as well as conflicts of interest.

The growth in size of the very largest consultants has properly led to increased concerns by clients over conflicts of interest. In its most simple expression, *how does a consultant ensure that sensitive information it received from one client is not transmitted to or even used to benefit a competitor,* now a client? The common answer has been that the giant firms take steps to separate people involved in such conflicting retentions, the so-called Chinese Wall. Another response is that the firms have in place review methods to ensure that they do not accidentally accept retentions when there is a current direct conflict, either in terms of working for a competitor or in terms of members of the consultant owning stock in competitors.

While this has been enough in the past, neither of these responses seems as satisfactory today:

- As for the Chinese Wall providing protection, many of the same firms now brag that they are involved in developing knowledge engineering/knowledge management programs. These efforts are designed to extract all learnings from just such retentions and make them available to all other members of the firm. To state the process is to state the problem.

- The capability of a firm's conflict-of-interest mechanisms to protect clients has come into question because of problems disclosed by the U.S. Securities and Exchange Commission. In a report on one of the largest accounting firms in the world, dealing with auditors' independence—that is, disclosing the ownership of investments in clients—an investigator for the SEC reported that "a substantial number of [the firm's] professionals, particularly partners, had violations of the independence rules, and that many had multiple violations. The review found excusable mistakes, but also attributed the violations to laxity and insensitivity to the importance of independence compliance. According to the independent consultant's report, [the firm] acknowledges that the review disclosed widespread independence non-compliance that reflected serious structural and cultural problems in the firm."[6] If such mechanisms are not working in the very sensitive area of accounting and audit assignments, what assurance is there that they are working any better in consulting situations?

MANAGEMENT CONSULTING AND ACCOUNTING

The ability of a consulting arm of an accounting firm to do business with a client of the accounting firm is a cause for concern. Some outsiders suggest that the presence of the consulting relationship might compromise an audit, but there is no direct evidence of that.[7] However, such concerns

(Continued)

(Continued)

are still heard from a number of quarters, including the SEC. Those worries are based on the fact that auditors often are expected to cross-sell consulting services, and may even receive a part of their compensation based on that. Critics wonder if those conducting an audit will be willing to challenge a client to whom they are trying to promote consulting services.

For these reasons, firms that deal with the same firm for audit and consulting services have developed a variety of approaches to avoid the appearance of a conflict of interest. Among them are the following:

- If consulting fees paid to the firm cross a preset threshold, such as 50 percent of the total fees paid the firm over a two- or three-year period, all of the contracts are reviewed by the audit committee of the board of directors.
- Projects where the consulting work deals with financial processes, such as accounts payable, are subject to stronger-than-usual project supervision by the client. The goal is to avoid having auditors placed in a position to review the work of their consulting peers.
- The firm does not use the consulting arm of the current auditor at all.[8]

Such concerns may have already provoked a response at the highest levels. In early 2000, it was reported that "three Big Five firms, however, have accepted, even embraced, the notion of spinning off their consulting businesses."[9]

In addition to a consultant currently working for a direct competitor, you should consider some other areas in determining whether a consultant is or will be placed in a conflict-of-interest situation. For example, if you answer yes to any of these questions, you may have created a conflict of interest for a consultant:[10]

- Can the consultant perform under the proposed contract in such a way as to devise solutions or make recommendations that would influence the award of future contracts to that same consultant?
- If the proposed contract requires some sort of support services, such as system engineering or technical direction, were any of the potential consultants involved in developing the system design specifications or in the production of the system?
- Has the consultant been involved in earlier work involving the same program, division, or activity that is the subject of the present contract where the consultant had access to information about your contracting intentions or to proprietary information that is not available to other consultants competing for the same contract?
- Will the consultant be evaluating a competitor's work?
- Does the proposed contract allow the contractor to accept its own products or activities on your behalf?
- Will the work under the proposed contract affect the interests of the consultant's other current clients (not just your competitors)?
- Are any of the potential consultants, or the personnel who will actually work on the contract, former employees of yours? If so, while they still worked for you, did they personally and substantially participate in the development of this contract, in the identification of your underlying needs, or in the purchasing of these same services in the recent past?

Answering yes to one of the foregoing does not mean you should not award the contract to the consultant, but it does mean that you should carefully consider the implications of awarding it before going forward. It would not be a bad idea to talk to management or the end user, or both, first to record any of your concerns before the contract is signed.

Interviewing

> "If you only hire consultants who make you happy, it is likely that you are doing nothing for your company, but everything for your ego."[11]

Whom Do You Interview?

Where time is not an issue, you might consider the selection procedure used by Williams-Sonoma, Inc. to limit the number of interviewees. Faced with the need to get assistance with respect to its move into e-commerce, it first contacted about fifteen firms. Then it gave each an RFP. Williams-Sonoma interviewed only the top three finalists. The final consulting firm, USWeb, prevailed over the other finalists, including IBM Global Services, because it demonstrated an understanding of the potential client's business as well as a mastery of its own discipline.[12]

Another option, if you are faced with a large number of potential candidates, is to seek a statement from them as to their qualifications to undertake an assignment *and* their ability to consider assuming the assignment. It makes no sense to consider a firm that cannot accept a retention because of a conflict of interest or unavailability of key staff when *you* need the assignment done. That means you should advise the consultants of any threshold limitations, such as the need to perform within a certain period of time or to work at a specific location. Then review the statements of qualifications and interest to determine which firms should be contacted for interviews.

How to Interview

> At Sears, a new CEO "kept three factors uppermost in his mind when he
>
> *(Continued)*

(Continued)

considered which consultants to hire.... First, the consultant had to have a demonstrated set of skills in the area under scrutiny.... Second, he demanded a commitment from the senior-level members of the firm to actively work on the engagement.... Last, he weighed the all-important 'intangible' factor—the fingertip feeling that he felt good about the person who would do the job."[13]

Your interviews can be on the telephone or in person. They may be as elaborate as interviewing each key member of the firm or requesting each firm to submit a complete proposal and price for the assignment. They can be as simple as reading about the consultant's experience and asking a few open-ended questions. But every candidate should be put through the same interview, even if it is a firm with which you have personally worked in the past.

When you are done, following up may be as simple as sending a contract to one consultant and asking whether the firm will sign it or as elaborate as giving each of the finalists an RFP to prepare.

In general, when you conduct these interviews, try to ask open-ended questions rather than specific, focused questions. Your goal is to understand the consultant's ability, competency, working relationships, record of keeping schedule, and ability to meet expectations.

In initial discussions with potential consultants, you should begin by presenting the problem or assignment directly to the consultant. That a consultant understands the problem and says that it can solve it is not enough. Although you may feel limited in evaluating the consultant's ability (because you cannot solve the problem yourself), there are several items you should discuss in order to decide whether to retain a particular consultant. These include:

157

- General information about the consultant and his or her experience.
- Specific information about key individuals employed by the consultant who would be working on the project. It cannot be overemphasized that if you are hiring individuals with particular experience, you should always assure yourself that those individuals will be the ones working on your particular problem.
- The consulting firm's experience in similar areas. With whom has it had this experience? What solutions has it created for other clients similarly situated? What was the cost-benefit ratio of the solutions proposed? Did its clients accept and implement the solutions?
- Whether the consultants strengths are in the strategic or in the tactical solution of problems.
- The consultant's references, other than clients or completed projects.
- Whether the individuals to be assigned to your project have worked on similar projects for other clients.

> "There are some lessons to be learned from [the] sad story [of Figgie International]. Beware of consultants marketing buzzwords.... They are usually peddling vague concepts that can't be measured or judged."[14]

Interviews will be as different as the consultants, the client, and the potential assignment. However, you should make sure that you cover at least the following issues:

- Exactly what business areas/industries has a consulting candidate worked in? That is an issue if you want someone who knows your business or industry. But remember, that is not always the case.

Sometimes you want or need the perspective an outsider brings to you, or you are hiring a consultant for its broad technical or professional expertise (such as networking or competitive intelligence), rather than industry-specific experience.

- What is the consultant's probable approach to the problem? Does the consultant seem to have an official or unofficial allegiance to one concept, one vendor, or one product? While offering systems or concepts based on one idea or piece of software is not necessarily bad, make sure that the consultant is not selling a preselected solution to your problem.
- Does the consultant charge you for proposals and estimates? While this is rare, it is not unheard of. In some practices, such as IT consulting, the work that goes into preparing a proposal or estimate is so considerable and entails such depth of investigation that the consultant is, essentially, starting the assignment when it delivers a proposal.
- Who will actually be assigned to the project? What are their skills and backgrounds? That is, can they do the job? Remember, *it is not the firm that will work on the retention; it is people from the firm.*
- What is the firm's reputation and background?
- What do your firm's evaluations say? Are they current? Are they based on the personnel with whom you expect to work or on partners and staff no longer there?
- Does the consultant seem capable of doing this project in terms of its size and relative workload? This does not mean that you must select a large firm. Rather, it means that the particular firm must be able to handle your project when you need it done.
- Do the references provided by the consultant check out? Was that work relevant to what you are trying to accomplish?

Hint: If you expect to discuss conflicts of interest or matters of competitive sensitivity with potential consultants, ask them to sign a basic confidentially agreement first. Otherwise, anything you say or show to them in the process of interviewing them is not protected.

You and the consultant should also discuss frankly exactly what the consultant will need from you. This should cover not only fees and costs but also your commitment of other resources, such as your time or the time of other key employees and executives. You must be frank in deciding whether you are willing and able to commit your time or that of others, particularly if you are overcommitted already. If you cannot or will not commit the resources required by the consultant, you may have to consider a radical change in the nature of the work to be performed.

What to Look For

"A research manager at IT industry researcher International Data Corp ... says potential clients should beware of consultants who are promising too much. 'Even some of the Big Five have made this error and had to either pull out, pay a penalty, or they got sued. As a client you have to look out for not being pulled in by enthusiasm that isn't properly backed up by past experience and case studies,' she says. Ask for proof that consultants can deliver what they promise."[15]

First, look for competence and ability. Can the consultant do the job that you have? Eliminate the ones who do not pass this test. Then, look for signs that you and the consultant can, or cannot, work well together:

160

- Does the consultant listen to you and understand what you are saying? Are his or her questions relevant?
- Does the consultant directly answer your questions during your interviews? If so, you should feel comfortable that the consultant will be direct during the retention.
- Do you think that the consultant is either avoiding an answer or trying to steer every question to the same response? In that case, try to determine why. Are your questions too vague? Are you asking the consultant to solve your problem then and there? Or is it because the consultant is not right for the project?
- Do you need other qualities, such as flexibility? If so, how do you and your associates who will work with the consultant rate the interviewees on these criteria?
- Will the consultants you initially meet with and interview be the same ones working on your project? If not, how will those working on the project be selected? Will you have the right to ask for replacements if you are unhappy with their experience or performance?
- How do you expect the consultants to work—with your personnel or on their own? Do they seem suited to and experienced in working that way?
- Does the consultant seem more interested in the likelihood of expanding this retention or in future retentions than in this project alone?

"Some firms will sell change management as a kind of communication tool; a hub or focus for multiple angles of attack [resulting in simultaneous sales of services from a variety of consulting arms]."[16]

Making the Selection

If one candidate is clearly the very best, you might want to retain that firm or individual at the end of the interview process. However, that rarely happens. If you did your search well and conducted your interviews fairly, you should end up with about two to five candidates. You may want to ask them for proposals or quotations (see Chapter 4).

> "When consultants are pitching business, the 'we' in 'We promise to make you well' is always an interesting thing.... My old firm is selling my experience even though I am not there, and they are selling it over and over again!"[17]

Whatever your decision, be comfortable with it. For some retentions, you want the most focused specialist available; for others, you need a mixture of specialism and broad perspective. *It is rare indeed that you want someone who brings nothing to the retention but a broad view of the horizon. That is a motivational speaker, not a consultant.*

Policy Statement: Similar Work

The following paragraph is designed to provide a very special benefit to the larger client. It requires that the manager seeking to retain any consultant must first make certain that no other client unit is having similar work done now or has had such work done in the past. The thought is that if similar work is under way, the manager may want to consider approaching the consultant already under another contract. The manager would then determine whether that consultant can or should perform the new, related duties efficiently and without interfering with its current work.

162

Prior to retaining any outside consultant, the Manager in charge of the assignment will determine that the same or substantially similar work has not been done or is not now being done elsewhere in [the Client].

[*Optional for companies with a consulting information center:* This can be done by contacting *name/position.*]

If similar work has been performed, a good manager should review that past effort. A manager may find that his or her new project has been done either partly or entirely. Even when that is not the case, the manager may want to review the past work and reports to learn from them. He or she can learn how to specify the services needed, how better to supervise such a project, or how to select a consultant for the current project. Management may find that the consultant who worked for the company earlier should be added to the list of those being considered for the new project.

NOTES

1. Kevin Kelly, "Group Therapy," *Business Week*, November 8, 1999, F48.

2. Nolan, "Six Laws."

3. Ripkin and Sayles, *Insider Strategies for Outsourcing Information Systems*, 25.

4. O'Shea and Madigan, *Dangerous Company*, 256.

5. Kyle, "Finding a Way."

6. U.S. Securities and Exchange Commission, "Independent Consultant Finds Widespread Independence Violations at PriceWaterhouseCoopers," Release 2000-4, January 6, 2000.

7. Stephen Barr, "Breaking Up the Big 5," CFO, May 2000, 54.

8. Barr, "Breaking Up the Big 5," 54, 63.

9. Barr, "Breaking Up the Big 5," 54, 64.

10. Based on Office of Federal Procurement Policy, "Management Oversight of Service Contracting," Policy Letter No. 93-1 (reissued May 18, 1994).

11. Geddes, "How to Get the Expertise You Lack."

12. Leon, "Client View."

13. O'Shea and Madigan, *Dangerous Company,* 136.

14. O'Shea and Madigan, *Dangerous Company,* 71.

15. Gary Abramson, "Their Pain, Your Gain," *CIO Magazine,* October 15, 1998, http://www.cio.com (September 28, 2000).

16. Lewis Pinault, "Consultants: Change Agents from Hell," *Upside,* March 2000, 182, 184.

17. Anonymous, "Confessions of an Ex-Consultant," 107, 110.

8

BEGINNING THE CONSULTING RELATIONSHIP

WHICH OF THE 10 RULES APPLY

From the Top 10 Ways to Make Sure You Do NOT Get Value from Your Consulting Relationships (The More You Do, the Less Value You Can Be Sure You Will Get):

- Don't ever talk about time or money.
- Get it started with a handshake. You can always do the paperwork later.
- Don't worry about defining what are to be the deliverables or how to measure them.

When you have decided on the right consultant, you and the consultant still have several points to deal with.

While they may sound simple, as with so many other issues you must deal with them at the beginning, in the contract, before the consultant begins the retention. They are:

- What is the relationship and who is in it?
- What is the consultant expected to do?
- How can the parties change their agreement?
- Where do the parties send their paperwork?

THE PARTIES

The opening of a contract should immediately identify the parties and set forth the entire context of the agreement. For easy drafting, you should abbreviate the full name of the client in some way after first identifying it. The same is true for the consultant being retained. One way to do this also helps ensure that the relationship properly characterizes that of an independent contractor. That is to refer to the firm being served as "the Client" and the other firm, such as CMV & Associates, as the "Consultant."

This contract sets forth the terms and conditions under which The Multinational Service Company ("Client") proposes to use the services of CMV & Associates ("Consultant") to perform work or services ("Work") described in Attachment A [alternate: in the Consultant's Proposal of October 1, 2000], which is incorporated into this contract. The Work is to be performed by the Consultant on the following terms and conditions:

For the retention of a consultant on a continuing basis, language such as the following is sometimes used:

> Appointment. I am pleased to confirm your
> appointment as a consultant to [the Client].

But it says nothing about what the consultant is to do. If the Client intends that retention to be on a continuing basis, it should add language on work and rates.

> Your compensation will be at the rate of $[amount] per [hour] [day] and will be based on the submission of Certification of Work Forms (enclosed) on a monthly basis. You will be paid at the same time you are reimbursed for approved expenses.

Such language provides that the consultant must keep the client informed of the progress of any work being performed under the agreement. This actually serves several purposes:

- It apprises the client of progress on the project to ensure that the consultant is working on it on a regular basis.
- It forces the consultant to keep the project or client-consultant relationship constantly in mind so that the consultant's time does not become allocated elsewhere.
- It enables the client to reorient the consultant if the consultant is working in the wrong direction, is incurring extraordinarily large expenses, or is devoting an excessive amount of time to the project.
- It reminds both parties of the existence of the relationship on a regular basis.

167

Such a clause can be critical when a client has retained a consultant on a continuing basis and does not utilize the consultant for an extended period of time. The consultant may use this clause to keep the client apprised of the fact that there is still a contractual relationship between the two parties to which the client should be paying attention.

Consultants may be retained on a number of different bases. One common basis is to serve in connection with a particular project the client is engaged in. If the project is of a fixed duration or otherwise clearly identifiable, the paragraph that follows is appropriate.

> I am pleased to confirm your appointment as a consultant to [the Client] to serve in connection with the [named] project.

Basically this means that as long as the project identified is underway, the consultant can expect to be working for the client on that project.

If a project is not easily identifiable, a consultant should not be hired by reference to the project but should be retained on another basis, say for a specific term. In that case, this clause may be used:[1]

> Term. I am pleased to confirm your appointment as a consultant to [the Client] for the period [dates].

In this situation, the parties should both be aware that no extension of the agreement is possible except in writing. Both parties should realize that if the consultant continues to perform services for the client after the term of the agreement has passed, the parties may not be operating under the agreement they signed. In fact, they may find that their practices, as well as the common law, have significantly changed the agreement they both believed existed between them.

SERVICES TO BE PERFORMED

One of the most common causes of problems in the consulting relationship is the failure to define clearly the work to be performed before any work has begun. One way to begin to define the scope of the task is to have the consultant prepare a written proposal, which then can be modified in negotiations and the final results incorporated into the final agreement.

If appropriate, the agreement should cover such matters as regular work reports and should, if possible, specify the expected results of the consultant's performance. The client may wish to specify also that it will do business only with a partner or principal of the consulting firm. Although the consultant has an implied legal obligation to do the work diligently and in a reasonably skillful way, the client is well advised to set standards of performance if there are objective ones that it can use.

The obligations of the consultant to serve and the client to pay must not be illusory, or the agreement will not be a valid, enforceable contract. A promise by the client to employ the consultant as long as it suits the client is regarded as an illusory promise because it cannot be enforced by the consultant. In contrast, an agreement providing that the consultant will perform all services of a certain described nature that the client decides need doing is not illusory.

The definition of the nature of the services that the consultant will provide to the client is very important. This is not an easy task, but failing to do it correctly can be very costly. Too often, parties to a consulting relationship leave

169

the nature of the services to be specified after the fact. Instead, they fall back on form language, talking in terms of "directions to be given" by the corporation and specific matters "to be agreed on at a later date." This approach is decidedly unsatisfactory from the standpoints of creating the relationship and of managing it. In addition, from a legal standpoint, it may be unsatisfactory because it is too vague. The more vague it is, and the more the consultant and client rely on "to be agreed on later," the more likely it is that if there are difficulties, a court might find either that there is no evidence that the parties even entered into a contract or that the relationship they intended was that of an employer and employee, with all the problems that creates.

Bad Example: The need for clarity and precision in a description of the work to be done can be illustrated by an old contract dispute with the federal government. In the mid-1970s, the U.S. Office of Education (OE) looked for a consultant. The task was described as developing an interpretive structure model based on "an analysis of resources for environmental education and studies." The consultant the OE ultimately selected submitted a 45-page proposal, which the OE accepted. The consultant then delivered his first progress report, as required by the OE contract.

The OE described these papers as "unintelligible." It then decided to terminate the contract on the grounds that the consultant had defaulted because the consultant had not done what the contract required. The OE also tried to force the consultant to repay the money he had already collected. Eventually, the OE agreed to *pay* the consultant about 50 percent of the total contract price to settle the case and get out of the contract. The reason for the OE's change of position was that there was no clear understanding of the

(Continued)

(Continued)

work to be done. As the OE's own contract officer put it, "How can we say they defaulted when it was never clear what we were expecting?"

To avoid unintended consequences, then, both parties should set forth as specific a description of the work or services to be performed as is possible. That description may be prepared initially by the consultant or by the client, or it may emerge through the process of discussion and negotiation.

If the client has a standard consulting agreement or purchase order that it uses, the parties may draft the description as an attachment. You can also use the attachment method when a consultant submits a written proposal or bid: The document submitted by the consultant can become the description of services or work to be performed.

The Consultant will provide the services as described in [identify the document with some degree of specificity], which is attached to and made a part of this contract.

After both parties have agreed to the specific language of the attachment, the attachment should be dated and labeled to indicate that it is part of the agreement between the client and the consultant. The parties should sign, or at least initial, the exhibit, which should be physically attached to the agreement.

You should never leave the preparation of such an exhibit to some "later date":

- First, this omission may render the agreement void, since the parties have not really reached an agreement on the specific subject matter of the contract.
- Second, this leaves open for collateral negotiation issues that properly should be settled before the agreement is signed and work started.
- Third, when the parties try this, they are trying to incorporate by reference a document that did not exist at the time they signed the agreement. This is bad legal practice.
- Fourth, if the parties are unable to arrive at an agreement regarding a statement of the work, postponing it may only serve to conceal or suppress deeper, more fundamental disagreements on the nature of the work and the work product. That, in and of itself, should be a warning to the client.

There are other issues here, too. If the attachment contains terms or conditions in addition to the actual description of the work to be done, both parties should be very careful. For if any of these terms, such as payment terms or confidential information, differ in any way from the terms in the form contract or purchase order, the parties have created a conflict. The contract language of the proposal may be considered as having been incorporated into a document that also has language covering these terms. If the parties do not intend that the consultant's terms will apply, then they might provide as follows:

> The Consultant will provide the services as described in [identify the document with some degree of specificity], which is attached to and made a part of this contract. The terms of this contract, where in conflict with the [attachment] will apply.

Frankly, however, this is sloppy drafting. It would be better for the parties either to have the description of the work printed separately and then incorporated or to have it inserted into the form document at the appropriate place.

Some businesspeople feel that loose language in a consulting agreement is desirable because it allows room for both sides to maneuver. However, experience has shown that the dismal possibilities of unenforceability as well as future disputes over the exact scope of the work represent major risks to the maintenance of the client-consultant relationship.

In contrast, a clear, detailed statement of the work to be performed is absolutely indispensable to creating a valid, enforceable agreement. Any looseness in specifications should be intentional and adopted by both sides in full recognition of the business and legal risks involved.

Implications should be avoided; precise language should be used. For example, in an agreement where the consultant promises to provide services "as required and as the Client may direct," the consultant's duty to perform is, by implication, conditional on receiving a notice of instructions and being given a reasonable time to provide the services. And if the agreement makes no provision for the time of performance and the parties ultimately must go to court over this question, a court is then free to fix a "reasonable" time for performance. If the agreement defines the time even incompletely or imperfectly, however, a court will not be so free to attach its own notion of what is a reasonable time for performance; it will be limited by the agreement. The agreement therefore should define the time of performance if it is important to either the consultant or the client. The definition of performance should be done with great care and specificity.

MODIFICATION

The relationship between consultant and client can become quite informal, especially in agreements where the duties of the consultant are somewhat open-ended. Care must be taken that all potential modifications of the agreement, including instructions, are in writing. Oral modifications and instructions can cause problems both with the statute of frauds and with the necessary specificity of the consultant's duties. Suggested language dealing with this is found in Chapter 9.

NOTICES

Unless the Client shall specify otherwise in writing, notices, statements, and all other matters concerning the Work to be performed under the contract shall be addressed to the Client as follows:

[address]

Unless the Consultant shall specify otherwise in writing, notices, work requests, and all other matters concerning the Work to be performed under the contract shall be addressed to the Consultant as follows:

[address]

Any and all notices or other communications required or permitted by this Agreement, or by law, to be served on or given to either party by the other party shall be in writing. They shall be deemed duly served and given only on actual receipt by the party to whom they are directed.

In many places in the contract, the parties agree to exchange information in writing. A section such as this sample establishes the specific addresses and even the names of persons to whom notice should be given to conform to the contract. This version provides that all notices given in the agreement are to be in writing, a practice that should be followed given the problems discussed earlier with the statue of frauds as well as with change orders.

The last section of the sample says that any notices are considered served on the parties *only* upon their receipt. The purpose of this is to counteract a legal doctrine that can provide that certain notices are considered as having been given once they are put in the mail. In a consulting agreement that involves face-to-face communication between or among a limited number of people on each side, such formality is not always necessary. What is important is that the parties actually receive the communications that the other parties send, that they are clear, and that the receiving parties are able to act on them.

NOTE

1. If the consultant is being retained to undertake a particular task, then the parties should try and set a due date or date after which the consultant's services will not be needed.

9

KEEPING THE RELATIONSHIP MOVING

WHICH OF THE 10 RULES APPLY

From the Top 10 Ways to Make Sure You Do NOT Get Value from Your Consulting Relationships (The More You Do, the Less Value You Can Be Sure You Will Get):

- Let the consultant define the task or tasks and make sure that they get done.
- Let the consultant put someone on the project with whom you've never met.
- Don't worry about supervision and reporting. Remember, they are the experts and you are merely the client.
- Discuss the next stage of work (or better yet, another retention) well before this one is done.
- Don't worry about defining what are to be the deliverables or how to measure them.

"Staff turnover at Ernst & Young in Canada [in 1999] was 20 to 25 percent."[1]

Every consulting relationship is different. In some, the consultant will literally go away and return in a few weeks with a written report. At the other extreme, the client may find that consultant personnel in unexpected numbers seem to be living with the client's own personnel. But regardless of the huge range of services that consultants perform for their clients, several key issues will arise as the consulting relationship develops:

- Who is doing your work?
- Work requests.
- Cooperation and coordination.
- Keeping the consultant focused.
- Corporate opportunities.
- Getting ready for your results.

WHO IS DOING YOUR WORK?

When you hire a consultant, just who *are* you hiring? If you cannot answer that question, deal with it before the assignment is begun.

The Consultant Personnel Game

A major criticism leveled against consultants of virtually every stripe is that with the larger firms, such as McGonagle & Company, the last time you see the people who convinced you to hire them is when the contract is signed. It is said that only with the smaller firms, such as CMV &

Associates, can you be sure of getting the personnel that you think you hired.

That is not completely true. Yes, larger firms rely on the more senior partners, called the rainmakers, to bring in business rather than to manage it. And yes, they will staff the average retention with other personnel, many of whom you have not met. But that does not mean you are not getting the services you need.

Still, many clients are concerned that they get what they think they have purchased in terms of expertise and even personality.

"Strong emphasis needs to be placed on assuring potential clients that senior talent will be in charge of the projects—at least according to... the CEO of Mitchell and Company, a management consulting firm. He explains: 'On one occasion, a reluctant company hired us only after learning that I would head the project. The client was looking for a firm that would put its senior people on the assignment.'

"[His] advice can go a long way toward overcoming the bad experiences some companies have had working with Big Five consulting firms, who often sell their expertise and then place college graduates in charge of projects."[2]

Of course, you want to make sure you get what you have just bought. But what does that mean? *If you are buying the expertise of one person or certain people at a firm, will they be working on this particular assignment?* Not necessarily, unless you make certain of it.

"When the consultants gave you an estimate, they should have told you

(Continued)

(Continued)

how much time their more experienced people would be devoting to your project. Once you've met and approved of those senior consultants—generally the partners and the folks one or two steps below—nail down their weekly time commitments to your company in your contract. Then add a clause saying that you can remove anyone on the team if things go sour. You should also have thumbs-down rights on the replacements."[3]

While you may wish to ensure that you have some control over who does and does not work on the retention, you must be careful not to go too far:

- If you specify that only certain named persons will work on the assignment, you may accidentally make the consulting agreement into a personal services contract. That means if there should ever be a dispute between you and the consultant, you may find that you cannot bring a lawsuit for specific enforcement.
- If you have the absolute right to name who works on the retention, you could run the risk of converting the agreement into an employment agreement.

This is not to say that you, as the client, should not assert some authority over who works on the retention and who does not. If the identity and experience of the consultants assigned to your project are important, put that information in writing at the beginning of the retention. Without that, you may find to your dismay that the people you worked with to define the assignment will not be working on it. There is nothing wrong with dealing up front with the identity of who will work with you.

180

> " 'We put into the contract that no one comes on to a project without the approval of the team members, generally based on personal interviews and résumés,' says [the] vice president for finance and comptroller at Sea-Land Service Inc.... The condition serves as quality control from the beginning of the project through its completion, since there is bound to be turnover during a long project.
>
> "Price Waterhouse [now PriceWaterhouseCoopers] accepted those terms and was awarded Sea-Land's largest current IT project."[4]

Contracting Issues

One way a client can feel comfortable that it is getting the firm that it thinks it hired in a complex retention is to add a section dealing with the assignability of the agreement.

> This agreement is personal in nature and is not assignable by either the Client or the Consultant. Consultant may subcontract portions of its requested Work or services on approval of the proposed subcontractor by the Client. Such approval shall not relieve the Consultant of its responsibility under this agreement for the Work.

By making the agreement "personal", the client says that it expects this particular individual (or individuals named) to do the work, and no others to do it. When the consultant is employed because of his or her unique areas of expertise, by making his or her performance nondelegable, or personal, the agreement may become one for personal services. As discussed, agreements that are regarded as personal service contracts are difficult to enforce by a suit for an injunction. On the other hand, permitting the consultant to assign part or all of his or her performance could negate any other clause stating that the client will deal only with the principals or partners of the consulting firm.

The assignability of the contract is a separate but related matter. The sample clause provides that the agreement is not assignable by either the client or the consultant. Assignable means that someone else, even another firm, can do the work that the consultant has agreed to do. This type of clause stipulates that the client does not wish to have the agreement assigned by the consultant to another individual. This clause does allow the consultant to subcontract a portion of its work, but only with the client's approval. In a large, complex project, such as clause may be desired.

If the parties do not want the performance of an essentially simple project to be assigned, however, there seems to be little justification for permitting subcontracting. Of course, the quality of work of the subcontractor and its performance is the responsibility of the consultant; the fact that the client has approved the particular subcontractor does not relieve the consultant from its liability for failure to perform.

This optional paragraph makes the contract non-assignable but does allow subcontracting:

This Agreement is personal in nature and is not assignable by either the Consultant or the Client. The Consultant may, however, subcontract its services, in whole or in part, to others without the prior approval of the Client. The Consultant guarantees to the Client compliance by such other persons with the responsibilities and liabilities assumed by the Consultant in the Agreement [, provided that the limitations on the Consultant's

(Continued)

(Continued)

liability set forth in the Agreement constitute the aggregate limit of liability of the Consultant and its subcontractors to the Client and that the Client agrees to hold only the Consultant responsible for any failure to so comply]. The Consultant agrees that the Client will incur no duplication of costs as a result of any such subcontract.

Here the consultant guarantees that the subcontracted performance will comply with the agreement. The language in brackets is designed to link with a clause elsewhere in the agreement that deals with the consultant's liability. It expands the limitation of the consultant's liability to include the aggregate liability of the consultant and its subcontractors. This language also properly provides that the consultant will ensure that there is no duplication of costs as a result of its subcontracting activities.

Here is yet another variation. It provides that either party may assign its rights or delegate its duties as long as each gets the written approval of the other party.

Either party may assign its rights or delegate its duties under this Agreement with the prior written approval of the other party. Such approval shall not relieve the Consultant of its responsibility under the Agreement for the Work. The Consultant may subcontract portions of the Work without the prior approval of the Client, provided, however, that such subcontracting shall not relieve the Consultant of its responsibility under this Agreement for the Work.

This paragraph gives each party substantial flexibility and would be appropriate in more complex situations than would the previous versions. For example, the client hiring the consultant may not be the subsidiary for which the services actually are to be performed. Similarly, the consultant that signs the contract may not be the particular subsidiary in a consulting firm that does the actual work. This contract also protects the signing parties by saying that subcontracting responsibilities under the agreement do not change the liability of either party for adequate performance, both for the work under the contract and the payment of bills.

The next paragraph should be considered when the client anticipates that others besides an individual consultant will be involved in the performance of the agreement. This language binds those persons working for the consultant on the project, in whatever capacity, to certain protective provisions in the agreement, such as those dealing with the ownership of patentable products or the retention and delivery of documents.

> The Consultant, its employees, and all others whose services may be contracted for by the Consultant to assist the Consultant in the performance of the Work shall agree to be bound by the terms of paragraphs x, y, z, and aa of the Agreement.

Of course, if the contract is between an individual consultant and a client, such a paragraph is not needed, because the individual consultant already has agreed to be bound by all these provisions. The paragraph could be revised to allow the client to waive some of these requirements. That would be appropriate when the delivery of a work product from a subcontractor to the consultant and also to the client adds nothing to the project except additional expense.

An alternate paragraph provides that the consultant *may* assign the agreement to any "of equal responsibility" to the consultant.

> Assignments. With the prior written consent of the Client, you may assign this Agreement and the benefits and obligations under it to any person, including a corporation, of equal responsibility to you. The consent of the Client may not be withheld unreasonably.

It is unlikely that a client would be happy with this concept, even though it requires that the consultant disclose to the client substantial information about the assignee to permit the client to determine its responsibility. This disclosure should include who owns the assignee and who will be administering and performing under the agreement. The sample language also provides that the consent of the client may not be withheld unreasonably, thereby providing some flexibility to the consultant.

WORK REQUESTS

No matter how hard people try, they may not be able to define, at the beginning, all the things that the consultant is expected to do. In such case, the parties might want to consider using change orders. That is, the parties provide in the agreement that the work or services to be performed by the consultant may be changed from time to time by letter requests—that is, documents—sent to the consultant by the client.

> Services. You will perform such work or services as are
>
> *(Continued)*

(Continued)

set forth in Exhibit A, which is attached and made a part of this Agreement. The work or services to be performed by you may be changed by [the Client] from time to time by letter requests sent to you. You shall keep [the Client] informed of the progress of any work being performed under this Agreement.

The sample's third sentence is designed to make sure that the client knows where the consultant is focusing its efforts, particularly when the client has made changes in the work it may be doing. This kind of clause should deal with very narrow changes only. Any broad changes in the nature of the work or services performed should always be treated as an amendment to the contract. Language such as this should not be treated as an open-ended invitation to the client to add or delete major responsibilities under the agreement.

Also, since the contract's language allows the client to unilaterally change the work, both parties should consider whether the consultant *must* take each such order as it is given. If the consultant is entering into an open-ended relationship, it may need to have the right to manage its personnel's time to handle several clients effectively and professionally. Remember, you must always be careful to make sure that the relationship cannot be characterized as employer-employee. Thus, you may want the consultant to be able to opt out.

[The Client] shall have the right from time to time to request in writing that the Consultant perform additional consulting work (the "Work") by written

(Continued)

186

> *(Continued)*
>
> work requests, provided, however, that the Consultant
> shall have the right to refuse any work request by noti-
> fying [the Client] within ten (10) days after receipt of
> the written work request.

This kind of clause is also appropriate when a consultant is retained on an open-ended basis and the client uses
formal written requests to activate the agreement, such as
when a client retains an advertising consultant just to have
the consultant available. The client might pay the advertising consultant a fixed sum to be available, and would
also agree to pay him or her on the basis of work performed.
The client would activate this kind of contract by sending
a letter to the consultant requesting that he or she review
certain advertising materials or plan an advertising campaign. In this type of case the work may be adjusted or even
assigned by letter request.

> Appointment. I am pleased to confirm your
> appointment as a consultant to [the Client].
>
> Work. You will perform such work with respect to [area
> of expertise] as [the Client] directs in written requests.
> Such work will be billed to [the Client] on the following
> basis: [here set out rates, how expenses are handled,
> terms, etc.].

This is an open-ended relationship. The client should be
very careful in using the work requests. They should come
only from one or two people, should put a ceiling on time
and costs, and set due or delivery dates very clearly.

Unless [the Client] shall specify otherwise in writing, all requests for Work to be performed under this contract shall be made in writing by [name and/or title of one person with this authority] who shall, in all respects, be considered [the Client's] Representative under this contract.

Because the designated individual, the "representative," is an important person, in a long-term contract it is wise to specify an alternate representative so that the project is not delayed due to the absence or illness of the representative. In an extraordinarily long and complicated project, it may be necessary for the client to add additional language stating that it may designate additional persons to serve as alternate or substitute representatives. If the need for that designation arises, it should be made in writing and delivered to the consultant. This clause is probably only necessary in the most lengthy, complicated, and expensive projects.

In the event of the representative's absence or incapacity, [another name and title] is designated [the Client's] Alternate Representative. The Consultant will keep [the Client] or its Representatives informed of the progress of the Work being performed under this contract.

In addition, the overall times of performance and standards of performance should be established in the agreement rather than in the work requests.

Unless otherwise specified in writing, the work

(Continued)

(Continued)

requested in each written work request will be completed within [number] of business days from the date of the request. All work shall be performed [set forth specific standards, if possible].

COOPERATION AND COORDINATION

"For consulting firms, change management offers a secure way to continuously field large numbers of consultants through the greatest pyramid scheme in the industry. A typical...engagement will involve extensive interviews with key managers, some external competitive homework, an...off-site revival-style meeting of 40 or 50 top managers and a commitment by those managers to carry on the flame..., creating a cascade of trauma and strong-armed commitment."[5]

This next section of the contract addresses the question of working facilities. Some consultants will have to work on the client's premises. This might be a consulting engineer who has to examine a particular structure or progress on a particular job. Or it may be a management consultant coming in to evaluate work-flow processing and related issues in one part of the client organization. In these situations, the consultant needs a place to work and certain services provided by the client. If the client provides those, this type of language should be used:

Working Facilities. You will be furnished with such facil-

(Continued)

(Continued)

ities and services at [location] as are suitable for your position and adequate for the performance of your duties under this Agreement.

Alternatively the client may wish to list those services, such as duplication, faxing, and the like, that it will provide, and thus for which it will not be billed as an expense. If the client does not intend to provide facilities and services at all, language should be inserted here to make that clear.

If the consultant needs access to materials or data in the client's hands, that should be directly covered. In fact, in some cases, the client may have already done significant preparatory work. In those situations, it may want to give the consultant immediate access to those materials, if for no other reason than to save unnecessary duplicate spending.

Data and Materials. To provide for effective use of resources, the Consultant will be permitted to utilize materials and data already in the Client's possession. The Client will provide, on a timely basis, any additional materials or data requested to assist the Consultant in connection with this Assignment.

The second sentence is one more often sought by the consultant than inserted by the client. It ensures that the consultant will not find that its performance is slowed down, or even made impossible, because the client is unable to provide it with client materials or data.

As noted elsewhere, when soliciting a proposal or quotation from a consultant, the client should always try to deal with the issue of costs, or disbursements, up front.

The client should always advise a consultant, before the consultant prepares a quote or proposal, on any policies that will have an impact on its pricing. In addition to payment terms, such as 60 days net, this includes policies covering matters such as travel. For example, whereas a consultant may have its personnel fly business class on all international flights, it may find that its client pays for this only on international flights of more than, say, eight hours. So when the consultant bills for business class travel on a four-hour international flight, one of several things can happen:

- The client may refuse to pay that amount, citing its travel policy on reimbursements, and pay only the coach equivalent;
- The client may pay "this time," but demand that the agreement with the consultant be changed to comply with its policies; or
- The client may pay without challenging the cost, but find that its own employees begin to develop a bad attitude toward the consultant whose personnel get to travel business class when they cannot.

None of these are desirable situations.

"Make sure the project fits on the company's strategic agenda and won't compete for time, funds or staff with other projects. Otherwise both the consultants and the client staff assigned to the project will become frustrated, and costly consultants' hours will be wasted.

"Dale Anderson...has faced this challenge from both sides—during his decade as CIO at several companies and as a consultant at Arthur Andersen. In a classic example of competing agendas, consultants plan client training for a given week, but then someone from within the company comes in with another project and says they can't run training that week. 'Wasting a week of consultants' time is expensive and [counterproductive],' says Anderson."[6]

KEEPING THE CONSULTANT FOCUSED

Merely because the client and consultant now clearly understand *who* is to do *what* does not mean there are no more management issues to deal with.

Monitoring and Reports

The agreement with the consultant should always provide some way for the client to be able to monitor progress and, if necessary, to provide direction or special assistance periodically. You should be wary of any consultant who indicates that he or she will take an assignment and report back at the end but does not see any need to provide interim communications, progress reports, or other feedback. Be particularly wary if the consultant appears reluctant to keep in regular communication with you.

The ways in which monitoring can be done will vary from retention to retention. They can be as simple as having the consultant talk to a client contact every week or two for a few moments; they can be more advanced, such as requiring formal progress reports; or they may entail the establishment of a series of milestones. In the latter case, the client and consultant agree upon specific events or items that can be used to mark progress under the retention. For example, if the retention is one involving training, one milestone might be the preparation of a final course; the next might be the beta testing of the course; then the revision of the course; then the scheduling of the final training.

An emerging trend among sophisticated users of consulting services: "Define the objective, never lose control, and watch the outsiders like hawks because faulty advice can generate losses that dwarf the profits spawned by good counsel."[7]

If you are working with a consultant for the first time, or the assignment is one that will take a long time to complete, you may want to monitor the assignment as it is being done. However, if you anticipate doing that, make sure that the consultant is aware of it *before* the assignment is begun. Remember, from the consultant's standpoint, your firm's monitoring activities (or needs for regular reports) may increase the time the entire project takes or increase the effort that the consultant expends. That translates into fees and costs. For that reason, it is not fair to impose a substantial monitoring/reporting requirement *after* an assignment has begun.

Before making a decision pro or con on progress reports, keep several factors in mind:

- Pro: Progress reports let a client handle issues that, if not handled, could become problems at the end of the retention. For example, assume that the client expects that the principal of CMV & Associates will do most of the work on the assignment but sees that an associate is doing it on-site. A brief discussion at the first progress report may allow the principal of the firm to point out that the on-site work is the smaller part of the work; the bulk is off-site.
- Pro: By requiring progress reports you avoid having your work put at the bottom of the consultant's pile.
- Pro: Progress reports allow the client to fine-tune an ongoing effort, so long as both sides have provided for such in the contract.
- Pro: Progress reports give internal clients, that is, those affected by but not involved in the assignment, a better feeling that a retention is likely to be a valuable effort.
- Con: Progress reports take the consultant's billable time. And that means the consultant will be charging you more than it would if there were no such reports to be made.

- Con: Not all retentions have easily identifiable benchmarks, milestones, or targets that make progress reporting a way of not only supervising but also managing progress.
- Con: The ability to make a good report is not directly correlated to the ability to deliver an acceptable final product or service.
- Con: A progress report is not the same as progress.

Regardless of how progress is tracked, it is important that both sides of the retention hold to schedules and meet milestones.

The Next Retention

"[Lewis] Pinault [who has worked for a number of firms, including BCG, Gemini Consulting, Arthur D. Little, and Coopers & Lybrand] cautions that [the highest level of consulting project management] demands a combination of personal characteristics that not everyone possesses—or would want to possess. These personality traits include the willingness to go to extremes in terms of scruples and personal energy, with the oft-explicit goal of manipulating hapless clients' sense of vulnerability in order to wring every last drop of billing time out of the client-consultant relationship."[8]

Keep your attention, and that of your consultant, focused on the task at hand until it is done. Why is this an issue even worth mentioning? Well, if you and the consultant are looking toward the next retention, how closely are either of you watching this one?

Experience shows that this advice grows out of separate concerns:

- Having the client and/or the consultant fail to completely focus on the effective completion of a retention, by looking to more work, merely increases the chances that the initial retention will have problems.
- As the client, if this is the first time you have used this consultant, are you already sure that you want to use him or her again? You have not yet gotten to the end of this retention, so there is no way that you can be certain that you and your company will be satisfied with the results.
- For many consultants, after having obtained the first retention, the primary goal as a businessperson is not to complete it. Rather, it is to expand the relationship with the client.

Do consultants really shift their focus during a retention from the current one to the possibility of the next one? Yes. They are in business just as you are, and once a retention is agreed on, a part of them is mentally looking for the next client, the next retention, the next proposal. And that is completely understandable. For example, a current guide to the management consulting industry frankly notes that there are four basic steps in any consulting engagement. The last is the presentation, but

the final presentation does not necessarily mark the end of the project.... Most [management] consulting firms work diligently to extend projects, usually beginning to talk with the client about additional work as early as the second or third step of an engagement.[9]

However, there are indications that in some consulting contexts, this tendency can become extreme. For example, one former consultant put it bluntly:

When I was a consultant, I spent more time thinking about what I was going to sell the client next than the problem I was supposed to be fixing. *My goal was to stay inside forever.*[10]

CORPORATE OPPORTUNITIES

During the retention, a special relationship is created between the consultant and the client. The following paragraph is designed to address one often overlooked aspect of that relationship during the term of the agreement.

During the term of this Agreement, the Consultant shall promptly reveal to the Client all matters coming to its attention pertaining to the business of the Client.

This requires that the consultant bring to the client's attention all matters pertaining to the client's business during the term of the contract. This covers so-called "corporate opportunities." Corporate opportunities, broadly speaking, include any information that the consultant has discovered while engaged on the work of the client that will benefit the client.

PREPARING FOR YOUR RESULTS

As you get ready to receive, use, and evaluate the results of the retention, make sure that you are prepared to compare what you expect to receive from the consultant with what you finally receive.

- If you are expecting a report, be ready to compare the final report with the written proposal given to you by the consultant at the beginning of the assignment. Make sure you account for any later changes in the assignment due to requests that you made. Are those changes reflected in the final report? In what ways? If not, why not?

- If the consultant is providing services, rather than a report, identify those with whom the consultant is working. Then you will be prepared to find out from them whether they were satisfied with the consultant as well as with its work (these *are* different). For example, they should be ready to tell you whether the consultant was cooperative, prompt, and effective. They should prepare to identify what they and the firm gained from the retention. They should expect to be asked how the recommendations will be implemented. If they will not be implemented, they should be ready to explain why.

NOTES

1. Gibb-Clark, "Merged Firm Aims to Bring Best of Both Worlds," M1.

2. Seifert, "Hired Guns."

3. Ronald B. Lieber, "Controlling Your Consultants," *Fortune,* October 14, 1996, http://www.fortune.com/fortune/1996/961014 /sum.html (September 28, 2000).

4. Abramson, "Their Pain, Your Gain."

5. Pinault, "Consultants: Change Agents from Hell," 182.

6. Abramson, "Their Pain, Your Gain."

7. O'Shea and Madigan, *Dangerous Company,* 111.

8. Kim Shively, "The System Made Me Do It: Lewis Pinault's Consulting Demons," Vault.com's *Case Closed: The Career Newsletter for Consulting,* June 22, 2000, http://www.vault.com (June 22, 2000).

9. Biswas and Twichell, *Management Consulting,* 36.

10. Anonymous, "Confessions of an Ex-Consultant," 107–108 (emphasis added).

10

WINDING UP THE RELATIONSHIP

WHICH OF THE 10 RULES APPLY

From the Top 10 Ways to Make Sure You Do NOT Get Value from Your Consulting Relationships (The More You Do, the Less Value You Can Be Sure You Will Get):

- Let the consultant define the task or tasks and make sure that they get done.
- Don't ever talk about time or money.
- Get it started with a handshake. You can always do the paperwork later.
- Don't worry about supervision and reporting. Remember, they are the experts and you are merely the client.
- Don't worry about defining what are to be the deliverables or how to measure them.

THE CLIENT'S PERSPECTIVE

As the retention winds down, the client is typically concerned with seeing that the final work product, be it a report or advice, comes to it on time and within budget. It is predictably anxious to get the results of the retention and put them to immediate use. As a result, it is at this time, more than at any other, that disputes with the consultant about pricing, deliverables, or work can arise.

THE CONSULTANT'S PERSPECTIVE

As the retention ends, the consultant tends to be looking past the current assignment. Whether a large firm or a small one, it is looking toward the next retention. That retention may be with this client or with others. If the consultant's personnel on this retention are already committed to another upcoming retention, the pressure is on the consultant to get the work done and to get on to the next project. This can on occasion adversely affect the final product.

MANAGEMENT ISSUES

"Looking for an inexpensive fix, companies frequently pick up people between jobs who are selling themselves as consultants. They may have technical expertise but lack the broad skills necessary to operate independently of an organization or deal with a client relationship.

"They may fall short of a client's performance expectations, or worse, leave before the project is completed to pursue an attractive job offer."[1]

Several management issues should have been dealt with before this final phase to ensure that the consulting relationship ends properly, that each party is satisfied with the process, and that any potential disputes are either avoided or handled with the minimum of stress:

- Final reports and other work products.
- Appraisals and reviews.
- Confidentiality issues.
- Conflicts of interest.
- Term and termination.

Final Reports and Other Work Products

When the retention is over is not the time for a client to deal with what documents or work products it expects to get from the consultant. That matter should have been dealt with at the very beginning.

This is particularly true if the client has a policy that requires a report or similar document to be made available for others in its organization seeking consulting services to review. If the agreement did not provide for such a report when it was signed, a client cannot very well insist on one at the end.

Appraisals and Reviews

In companies where data on consultants is collected and shared, such data may have already been a powerful assist in selecting the right consultant or avoiding the wrong one. The manager who has benefited from some central file of reports or appraisals should not forget to continue to contribute to this effort. And the best time to focus on what the client needs to conduct is at the beginning; the best time to start the appraisal and review process is just as the retention is ending.

The manager should not leave an appraisal or review to be done well after the end of the retention, when he or she "has the time." Nor should it be done by someone other than the manager who approved the hiring and who was directly involved with the entire retention. To do so renders the entire process pointless.

Confidentiality Issues

A critical issue is what access the consultant will have to the client's information and how the consultant will handle that information. A related issue is how the consultant will treat the results of the assignment.

To perform effectively, in many cases a consultant has to have direct, continuing, and unimpeded access to a broad spectrum of corporate records and other information that is highly sensitive. The issue, then, has two elements:

1. Protecting the confidentiality of the client's information while the assignment is being conducted, and
2. In some cases protecting the client's information from being disclosed after the retention.

The key here is to have a clear understanding between client and consultant that the various kinds of data and information the client provides will be kept confidential and that even the results of the assignment being conducted for the client may also have to be kept confidential. In addition to articulating this requirement in the contract, look for the following as evidence of the consultant's ability and willingness to keep these kinds of commitments:

- How many people in the consultant's organization will actually know the identity of the client? How many will have access to the client's information and personnel?
- If the client provides the consultant with materials during the assignment, will they be returned uncopied?

- Do client names appear on copies of work kept by the consultant?
- What does the consultant do with the work files accumulated during an assignment? Are they kept intact, are they assimilated into a knowledge bank, or are they destroyed?
- Does the consultant name other clients and describe assignments conducted for them? Do you, as the client, want the consultant to refrain from doing that with your name and/or details of your retention?

Conflicts of Interest

Related to confidentiality concerns is the issue of conflict of interest. For many clients, the notion that a consultant is working for them and a direct competitor at the same time is inconceivable. But for consultants, it may be a very desirable situation.

The consultant very clearly wishes to have the greatest degree of flexibility in developing and servicing new clients, in addition to its current client. And its ability to do both things simultaneously may be seen by some as a welcome economy in operations, if nothing else. But consultants also often wish to be able to point to the results they have achieved for an identified client to recruit additional business, and, of course, benefit from its experiences with these clients.

The client, on the other hand, should be concerned about where and when its current consultant will deal with direct or indirect competitors. The client should specifically deal with issues such as confidential information and trade secrets, but there is more that the consultant takes away from a retention than that. The knowledge it derives from each assignment serves to build up its ability and expertise, which in turn make it a more marketable firm. But to what degree should that knowledge be immediately available to benefit your direct competitors? That is an issue that must be faced in many contexts.

Term and Termination

At the beginning of the retention, both sides should know, and clearly express in the agreement, when the retention will end:

- It may be when the project is completed, in which case the agreement should include at least an estimate of that date.
- It may be when a specific project with which the retention is linked is completed.
- It may be when one of the parties—if this is agreed on in advance—gives the other party notice that the retention is over.

It is in the interest of both parties to understand when or under what terms the retention will end.

POLICY ISSUES

Your company may have or want to develop specific policies dealing with consultant retentions.

Final Report

Company policy may require that information about what each consultant has done for the client (or a particular unit) is to be sent to a particular officer on completion of each assignment.

A copy of the final report of each outside consultant, or a summary of the services performed if no final report is prepared, will be forwarded to [name/position] on completion of each assignment.

This type of policy is aimed at collecting in one place information on the services provided by the client's consultants, a particularly critical matter in highly decentralized companies. One can easily imagine a situation where one unit of a client asks for certain kinds of market research services to be performed, and later that year, another unit of that client contracts for similar services to be performed by another consultant elsewhere in the country. The primary goal of the policy is to avoid duplication in contracting. However, this works only when and to the extent that managers check the repository of materials first.

By referring to the collected documents before entering into a consulting contract, managers can also gain a better understanding of precisely how to frame an assignment to be given to a consultant, as well as a standard against which to review the quality of the final product. This in turn can be significant if the contract with a consultant requires—as it should—that the final work product be acceptable to the client. Referring to similar reports by competing consultants may give a client a strong legal basis on which to reject a report as inadequate if the client has retained that right. These reports, in addition to preventing duplication in hiring, provide a library available for executive review.

Appraisals and Reviews

This next paragraph requires that a manager in charge of a consulting assignment prepare a consultant appraisal and review form. This form is then forwarded to a senior administrative officer for central access. A suggested form is included in this section. This policy, together with that set forth in the previous paragraph, should allow clients to determine whether consultants under consideration are competent, at least to the extent that they have performed acceptably on other assignments for the client.

The Manager in charge of the consulting assignment will prepare a Consultant Appraisal and Review Form at the conclusion of any assignment. This will be forwarded to [name/position].

One way to evaluate consultant services so that others within the company can benefit is to require a closing appraisal or review, which will be available to others within the company. This would tie into the suggested policy statements. The forms that could be used vary so widely that it is better to set out the broad areas to be covered and then let each manager provide his or her own remarks, responding to those areas.

CONSULTANT APPRAISAL FORM

Name and address of consulting firm retained:

Member of firm responsible for this account:

Dates retained: _____, 2001, through _____, 2001

Nature of assignment (check all applicable):

❏ Planning	❏ Employee benefits
❏ Taxes	❏ Marketing
❏ Organizational	❏ Regulatory
❏ Investments	❏ Product development
❏ R & D	❏ Strategy
❏ Personnel recruiting	❏ Supply chain
❏ Financial	❏ Customer relations
❏ Information technology	❏ Communications
❏ E-commerce	❏ Engineering
❏ Real estate	❏ Competitive intelligence

(Continued)

(Continued)

❑ Merger/acquisitions   ❑ Joint ventures
❑ Government relations   ❑ Other (specify):

Brief summary of assignment:
The members of the firm who supervised services provided by the Consultant were:

❑ Outstanding   ❑ Good
❑ Fair   ❑ Poor

Comments:

Other employees of the firm principally involved on this assignment were:

(Name)
❑ Outstanding   ❑ Good
❑ Fair   ❑ Poor

(Name)
❑ Outstanding   ❑ Good
❑ Fair   ❑ Poor

Comments:

The overall quality of service(s) provided by the firm on this assignment was:

❑ Outstanding   ❑ Good
❑ Fair   ❑ Poor

(Continued)

(Continued)

Comments:

The services of this firm should be:
❑ Used for future work in the following areas:
❑ Limited to future work in the following areas:
❑ Not used for any future assignments.

Comments:

(Signed)

In any appraisal, regardless of whether a form is used, the manager in charge of the retention should review and evaluate the retention from several different angles:

- First, the manager evaluates the services of the member of the consulting firm responsible for the retention of the account. Those services include such matters as supervision, consultation with the client, control over expenditures, and final presentation.
- Next, the manager evaluates other members of the consulting firm principally involved on the assignment. This typically includes junior partners in the firm or senior and middle-line associates (by whatever name). The purpose is to assist the client in

future relations with both this and other firms. For example, if the client manager felt the work product was good but the partner in charge of the account at the consultant did not exercise strong budgetary constraint, the manager could recommend that the consultant be used in the same area in the future but that a different partner be in charge of the account or retention. Similarly, if one or more of the consultant's employees are highly regarded by the client manager, a special note could be made of that. Why? The consulting industry often sees aspiring individuals leave major consulting firms to join smaller consulting firms or to establish their own businesses. By evaluating key consultants, the client manager can follow a particularly competent individual to his or her next place of employment and retain that firm in the future.

- Finally, the client manager needs to evaluate the overall quality of the service provided by the consultant on the assignment. This evaluation includes all the consultant's work as well as the two prior appraisals.

In evaluating the consultant's overall performance, the client manager should focus on three areas: (1) the nature of the assignment given to the consultant, (2) the working relationship established with the consultant, and (3) the results expected *at the beginning of the assignment.* The evaluation should consider at least the following broad areas:

- Did the consultant accomplish the *goals* set out at the beginning, as well as modified during the project, if they were modified?
- Were *changes* made in the nature of assignment? If so, why? For example, did the client fail to define the task, or was the consultant unable to perform as promised or desired?

- What, if anything, did client personnel *gain from working with the consultant?* Was that consequence intended or not? How beneficial was that exposure? Could that benefit have been acquired elsewhere at a lower cost?
- Was the project *completed?* If so, was it finished on time?
- How was the *final work product* delivered to the client? Was it clear and immediately usable, or did it have to be explained or reworked?
- Were the *solutions,* if any, proposed by the consultant responsive to the problems identified at the beginning? Were they practical, and will they be implemented? If they are not going to be implemented, why not?
- Was the *cost* of the project within the original contract limit or within initial cost estimates? If not, why was there a difference?
- Are the results of the project *beneficial* when compared with the project's final costs?
- Did the project leave any issues *unresolved* or *deferred* for further consideration pending implementation of the study? Why?

In preparing any evaluation, absolute candor is required. The client manager must be prepared to acknowledge where the client's own actions caused problems. For example, the final cost of a project may be higher than anticipated, but the reason may be the client's failure to cooperate promptly with the consultant. Just as the success of a project is claimed by all parties, the failure of a project may be the fault of all concerned. The client must have a good consultant, and the consultant must have a good client.

The client manager should specifically state whether the services of this consultant should be used for more work in particular areas, should be limited to work only in certain areas, or should not be used at all on any future assignments. Evaluations such as these are quite important and should be kept confidential. In addition to the manager's comments, a client policy might provide that a copy of the final report, if it is not too long, technical, or sensitive, be included with the appraisal form, so that individuals considering using the consultant in the future have a chance to review the work product.

Some companies that do a lot of business with consulting firms of all types have tried to control, indirectly, the way in which consultants are retained. They do so by using the services of a person such as the one receiving all of these appraisals. Managers considering using an outside consultant are then required to contact an inside expert for information on the track record of the firm under consideration, as well as suggestions for other possible consultants.

Before retaining any outside consultant, the Manager in charge of the assignment will obtain from [name/position] an appraisal of the consultant(s) under consideration as well as recommendations of other firms capable of carrying out the assignment. These will be based on any appraisals previously submitted, as well as on internal recommendations, outside references, interviews, and other searches for competent consultants not previously used by [the Client].

CONTRACTING ISSUES

When planning to manage the ongoing client-consultant relationship, it can be useful to deal with associated issues in the contract.

Reports and Work Products

A matter rarely dealt with in consulting agreements but one of real importance concerns reports and work products. A work-product clause can be designed to accomplish several ends. In the following sample, at the completion of the retention, the client that has paid for the project has full rights to all the work products it paid for. The paragraph clearly sets forth that the reports or the work products are to be delivered to the party that paid for them. If the parties are not able to complete the performance under the contract because of the consultant's inability, intervening acts, or even breach of contract, this paragraph gives the client the right to whatever work product the consultant has completed.

Report and work products. Any and all reports, manuscripts, and any other work product, whether completed or not, that are prepared or developed by you as a part of the work under this Agreement shall be the property of the Client and shall be turned over to the Client promptly at the Client's request or at the termination of this Agreement, whichever is earlier.

When a management consultant is brought in to study a problem, his work product, and in fact, some of his performance under the agreement, may be in the form of a written report. After the report is delivered and accepted, the contract has been fulfilled and the relationship is ended. A problem arises when, for any number of reasons, performance cannot be completed and the parties wish to terminate the relationship.

" 'I know of one organization that analyzed the cost structure of every steel company in Europe and then went and sold that research to every steel company in Europe,' notes [the worldwide managing director at Bain & Co.] 'When consulting firms put their people to work that way, it hardly creates a competitor-crushing advantage for their clients.' "[2]

If the client has expended moneys, it should have a right to the work in progress, whether completed or not. Without this clause, it is not certain that the client has that right. The clause gives the client the right to any and all reports, manuscripts, and any other work products, completed or not, that the consultant has prepared or developed as part of his or her work under the agreement. The insertion of this clause puts the consultant on notice that such materials must be kept separate from that of other projects.

This is particularly critical when a consultant is to prepare a survey of some sort—for example, studies in a certain field—and then is unable to complete the project. Even the partial notes of what the consultant has reviewed unsuccessfully may be of assistance to the client or another consultant in completing the project. The paragraph also enables a client to establish whether a consultant has in fact worked under the agreement, if there should be a dispute regarding compensation upon termination or breach of contract. Even if the consultant's work consists of providing a service rather than a report, these materials should be collected and given to the client. In the case of a consulting engineer, for example, the engineer's notes may be important to the client in the event of a lawsuit against the client arising out of the project. In such a situation, the agreement may stipulate that the consulting engineer will keep the originals of his or her notes and provide the client with a legible copy; this may protect the client if a lawsuit were to arise out of the work the engineer inspected and the engineer were not available to testify and validate his or her records.

This provision serves two other functions:

1. It ensures that the client will be able to transfer what it has paid for to a replacement or successor consulting firm.
2. It serves as a form of control over the activities of the consultant. Often, clients not used to using

consultants worry that consultants may not be progressing, as often there is no work product until a final report. The clause says that the client can request that the materials be turned over to them. This gives the client a way to check on the consultant's progress, if it is worried, and lets it feel more secure in paying for ongoing work by a consultant when it is unable to see a finished work product.

When a client is paying for materials to be used by the consultant, it may want to use the next clause to make sure that it at least has the right to get those materials that it is paying for.

Disbursements will be made for special services, such as express charges, out-of-the-area travel, and significant commercial printing/copying, as well as materials to be acquired in connection with work on this Assignment, such as purchased special reports and copies of reports filed with agencies of federal, state, and local governments, as well as copies of published articles. The Client has the option to receive all such materials.

Confidential Information, Trade Secrets, and Other Sensitive Information

"Once you've got them inside, I would never give a consultant any of my internal data. You don't want to read about your secrets on the Internet, and you certainly don't want your consultants giving them to your competitors.... I certainly wouldn't tell them what direction my business will head in."[3]

214

The sample confidentiality clause that follows is extremely broad. Note that it provides that the identity of the client is to be kept in confidence. Clients should realize that most consultants do not want to do this. While a referral from a satisfied client is a powerful business development tool, even being able to list that the consulting firm has served a group of clients with recognizable (or marquee) names is also of value.

> "Bain consultants didn't carry business cards. They used code names when discussing clients on airplanes. Bain didn't allow documents on desktops."[4]

A limitation such as this is found only in situations where the retention of the consultant itself is a competitively sensitive issue, such as in competitive intelligence. In that field, many clients properly believe that the fact that they have hired a competitive intelligence consultant, or even a particular consultant, is itself competitively sensitive information that they would rather keep from their competitors. A compromise might be that the "identity of the Client will not be disclosed without the Client's consent for a period of [time] following the end of the Retention."

> Confidentiality. The Consultant will not disclose to any person, firm, or corporation [the identify of the Client or] any confidential information regarding the Client, this Assignment, or the business of the Client received or developed in connection with this Assignment without the Client's consent.

The next contract sample deals with the sensitive area of confidential information from another direction. This is one of many clauses that the parties should discuss very carefully.

> In performing the Work, the Consultant may acquire or be made aware of certain confidential information, in particular, but not limited to, confidential information relating to the Work and regarding products, processes, and operations as well as present and contemplated activities of the Client. The Consultant, its employees, and others whose services may be procured by the Consultant to assist the Consultant in the performance of the Work shall not divulge or disclose such confidential information to others without first having obtained specific written permission from the Client to do so. The term "confidential information" as used here shall mean information disclosed to the Consultant by Client or information obtained by Consultant for the Client in the course of performing the Work hereunder, excluding (a) information previously known to the Consultant or information that is publicly known (except through disclosure by the Consultant in violation of this paragraph) and (b) information that comes to the Consultant from a third party without confidential commitment.

If the client is concerned about a particular kind of confidential information, it should specify that in the last sentence of the paragraph. There it would note that confidential information means certain information "including, but not limited to," the special category of information about which it is concerned, such as customer lists. This is important because many consultants must have access to extremely confidential information. In some cases, they have and need access to confidential information that is available to only a few employees or officers of the client. In fact, in performing consulting services, the consultant may have access to information unavailable to anyone below the COO or CEO. That means the client needs a nondisclosure agreement. Without one, the only protection the parties have is common law or statutory protection of information generally known as trade secrets.

Confidential information could include salary scales, development plans for new markets, studies on acquisitions or entry into new fields, and other information that does not bear directly on the day-to-day business of the client. Trade secrets are a much more limited category of information than confidential information. Trade secrets usually include customer lists, unpatented manufacturing processes, and instructions to marketing forces. What is important to know is that *for a Client to rely on the protection of trade secret law, it must have already identified the information as a trade secret and have a program in place to keep it protected.* The following type of clause deals with implementing an existing trade secret protection program with respect to the consultant.

In performing the Work, the Consultant may acquire or be made aware of trade secrets of the Client. The Consultant, its employees, and others whose services may be procured by the Consultant to assist the Consultant in the performance of the Work shall not divulge or disclose such trade secrets to others. The term "trade secret" as used here shall mean any information, including a formula, pattern, compilation, program, device, method, technique, or process, designated by the Client as a trade secret.

Because a trade secret is a very narrow class of data, the parties should not rely on the trade secret laws to cover any other types of sensitive information. Rather, they should handle those cases specifically. For example, what if the consultant is to be given copies of particularly confidential materials that must be used off-site? These might be salary schedules or succession plans. In any case, the agreement should state that the client agrees to deliver this information to the consultant *and* that the consultant agrees not to make or retain any copies but to return the document or documents directly to the client.

A client may desire additional or different confidentiality protections. For example, during a retention, a client may be giving the consultant access to, and permission to copy, sensitive internal materials. Caution dictates that if the materials are sufficiently sensitive, the consultant should be required to return them to the client. For particularly sensitive materials the client may wish to have the consultant agree in writing that "no copies of, or confidential data found in, any Client materials will be retained following the end of the Retention." This is something that should be of concern, particularly as the larger consulting firms begin to advertise that they are engaged in data mining. In those situations, the client "learnings" are no longer kept from competitors by the classic Chinese Wall but may well become a part of the firm's common knowledge base. If this is an issue, you, as the client, would be well advised to have the consultant specifically brief all those serving on the retention as to this requirement.

Unless otherwise agreed, all materials provided to the Consultant by the Client will be returned to the Client at the conclusion of the Assignment and the Consultant will retain no copies of such materials.

The next question is: How long is information that is specifically designated as confidential to be kept in confidence? The sample paragraph that follows attempts to protect information received by the consultant from outside disclosure for a period of years. It is virtually impossible and quite improper to bind the consultant forever in its use of all information received from the client. Various state laws and federal laws protect the client against the disclosure of certain kinds of trade secrets. A confidentiality clause covers additional information. But the consultant may have access to materials not traditionally regarded as trade secrets or covered by a confidentiality clause the disclosure of which may be damaging to the employing client, at least for a period of time.

> The Guinness litigation and prosecutions in Britain in 1990 "showed how much damage a consultant can do if the sensitive inside information he needs to do his job falls into the wrong hands once a relationship sours."[5]

In setting the number of years for which the agreement will apply to all other information and communications, the parties should be realistic and deal with the potentially damaging nature of information to which the consultant may have access.

> During the term of this Agreement, and for [number] years after the end of this Agreement, unless required by law to do so, without the written consent of the Client, the Consultant shall not reveal to outside sources any matters the revealing of which may, in any manner, adversely affect the Client's business.

Three to five years should cover most manufacturing and service industries. Remember, trade secrets or other specific confidential information, to the extent that such matters exist, should be covered elsewhere.

It is important for both parties to remember that for any restrictions on information to be effective, not only must the persons signing the contract know of the restrictions, but it is imperative that all persons involved in the retention (on both sides) be told specifically of the restrictions and their importance.

CONFLICTS OF INTEREST

During the agreement, a special relationship is created between the consultant and the client. We have touched on that in our discussion of the handling of confidential and other types of information. The following paragraph addresses a related matter. A client may desire an additional level of protection for confidentiality concerns and may limit its consultant's contact, at least during the retention, with competitors. It is better to list the firms for which the consultant cannot work during the retention than to rely on a general statement, such as the first option in brackets.

> The Consultant represents that, during the course of the Assignment, it will not be working for [a direct competitor of the Client] [any of the following firms: list of firms].

Another, less specific, approach is as follows:

> During the term of this Agreement [and for xxx months thereafter] the Consultant shall not accept similar employment from, or serve in a similar capacity with, any other concern that is at such time engaged in a business of a like or similar nature to the business now being conducted by the Client.

Under the preceding clause, the consultant may not accept similar employment from another concern engaged in a similar business during the term of the agreement or for a period after the agreement is over. This is somewhat different from a "noncompete" clause, which keeps the consultant from working for a competitor after the agreement is over. As indicated earlier, noncompete clauses can be difficult to enforce and so should be used only in the most extreme circumstances. The same is true for this conflict-of-interest clause. Just as with a noncompete clause, the conflict-of-interest clause should be limited both in term and scope.

TERM AND TERMINATION

The best time to deal with ending the client-consultant relationship is *before* it begins.

General Concepts

Any unwritten agreement that cannot be performed within one year may run afoul of the statute of frauds. Thus, any consulting relationship should be created in writing for a stated term. In drafting a duration clause, specificity is again necessary, as an agreement stating that the contract is to last "so long as conditions warrant" may be too indefinite for enforcement.

Further, the manner in which the term is stated can have varying consequences. For example, if a consultant who has an agreement with option periods exercisable by him or her is discharged wrongfully, the client may be liable for the present value of the unexpired term of the agreement plus all option periods. A contract renewable at the client's option or by mutual agreement therefore is preferable to one renewable at the consultant's option.

If the client has no use for the consultant's work after a certain date, the client should insist that it be released from the contract if the consultant's performance has not been rendered satisfactorily by that time.

It is not unusual for a commercial contract to state that it can be terminated for "good cause shown." Using such terminology invites lawsuits, however, because the existence of "good cause" may be a question that can put a case directly to a jury. The grounds for termination should, where possible, be categorized or defined fully.

Some agreements include an "option to cancel." The power this provision creates is not generally made conditional upon the client's dissatisfaction with the results; it is a power to cancel if and when the client desires. Such a power does not mean the contract is illusory. No action for breach of contract can be maintained against the client if it has exercised this power to cancel in accord with its terms and otherwise has complied with the contract. Making an analogy to the law of employment contracts, when an agreement provides that the consultant's performance must be to the client's satisfaction, a court will not inquire into the reason for the termination under this clause as long as it is made in good faith. That is, the client must in fact be dissatisfied; its dissatisfaction does not have to be reasonable.

A clause providing for automatic termination upon the occurrence of a specified event generally is to be regarded as giving either party an option to terminate the agreement by giving notice to the other party of the event. Upon receipt of that notice, the contract is terminated.

The notice required for termination should be discussed in the agreement. If the agreement is not for a fixed term and is thus able to be terminated at will, there is no general legal principle that requires notice of a specified length of time. As was indicated earlier, all notices and instructions should be in writing. The agreement should provide how notice is to be given, to whom it is to be given, and how much in advance it must be given.

Contract Options

Termination as provided for in the following paragraph is fairly standard in open-ended retentions, but *not* in project-oriented assignments.

Termination. This Agreement may be terminated upon [thirty (30)] days written notice by either party.

The client should determine whether it wishes the agreement to be terminated on notice or not. It may wish the agreement to be terminated upon its notice, particularly when the agreement is for a period of time and not for a particular project. It is unlikely that a client will want the consultant to be able to terminate on less than 30 days' notice. In fact, the client may wish that the agreement may be terminated by the consultant on 30 days' notice only if the consultant provides an acceptable substitute to the client who will assume the responsibilities of the consultant under this project.

This following paragraph is a termination clause that gives broad powers to either party to the contract. It is aimed at a relationship wherein the consultant is carrying on a variety of assignments. It allows either party to back out of the agreement at any time, providing that projects then under way are completed. It also permits one party or the other to suspend performance temporarily under the agreement.

Notwithstanding any other provision of the agreement,

(Continued)

(Continued)

either the Client or the Consultant may cancel this
agreement on written notice to the other party,
provided, however, that the Consultant may not
terminate any Work requested by the Client and not
rejected by the Consultant as provided for in paragraph
X of this agreement before the Consultant's notice of
termination [, unless the Client shall so consent]. The
Client may, however, direct the Consultant to terminate
any Work at any time, or the Client may suspend the
Consultant's performance temporarily or on a specific
project under this agreement at any time. The Client's
only obligation under this paragraph for any such cancellation, cessation, suspension, or redirection of the
Work being performed by the Consultant shall be the
payment to the Consultant of the fees and authorized
expenses for the Work actually performed.

The last portion of the sample provides that if the client
exercises its power it is only liable to pay for the consultant's actual expenses and fees to date. This eliminates any
obligation to the consultant for profits that the consultant
might have anticipated in completing the work. *This type of
clause should not be used in every situation, as it may not
be in the interest of either the client or the consultant to permit such broad termination or suspension privileges.*

This type of language is certainly not appropriate in a
contract between a client and consultant governing the performance of a single project of limited scope to be done
within a limited period of time. In such cases, this paragraph should not be used.

Another version of this clause allows either party to
cancel the contract on written notice to the other. It also
provides that the client may direct the consultant to terminate any work under the contract or to suspend its work.

The clause permitting *mutual* cancellation is more common than the unilateral termination clause just discussed. Given the fact that either party can cancel the entire contract, it would be unusual for the consultant to not agree that the client can terminate only a portion of the consultant's work under the contract. Realistically, this clause is designed to be exercised only when the consultant's work depends on other projects that have been halted for one reason or another. In addition, such a clause might be appropriate when the consultant is being paid by the project, so that failing to complete the contract leaves the parties without an agreement on what the consultant should be paid.

Notwithstanding any other provision of this Agreement, either party may cancel this Agreement on written notice to the other party. On written notice, the Client may direct the Consultant to terminate any of the Work at any time, or the Client may suspend, temporarily, the Consultant's performance under this Agreement at any time or from time to time. The Client's only obligation under this paragraph for any such cancellation, cessation, suspension, or redirection of the Work being performed by the Consultant shall be the payment to the Consultant of the fee for the Work actually performed.

NOTES

1. Kyle, "Finding a Way."
2. Lieber, "Controlling Your Consultants."
3. Anonymous, "Confessions of an Ex-Consultant," 107, 112.
4. O'Shea and Madigan, *Dangerous Company*, 225.
5. O'Shea and Madigan, *Dangerous Company*, 244.

11

DISPUTES, LAWSUITS, AND COMPLAINTS

WHICH OF THE 10 RULES APPLY

From the Top 10 Ways to Make Sure You Do NOT Get Value from Your Consulting Relationships (The More You Do, the Less Value You Can Be Sure You Will Get):

- Let the consultant define the task or tasks and make sure that they get done.
- Don't ever talk about time or money.
- Get it started with a handshake. You can always do the paperwork later.
- Don't worry about defining what are to be the deliverables or how to measure them.

THE CLIENT'S PERSPECTIVE

As the retention winds down, the client is typically concerned with seeing that the final work product, be it a report or advice, comes to it on time and within budget. It is predictably anxious to take the results of the retention and put them to immediate use. Thus, it is at this time, more than at any other, that disputes with the consultant about pricing, deliverables, or work can arise.

THE CONSULTANT'S PERSPECTIVE

As the retention is ending, the consultant, whether it is a large or small firm, tends to be looking past the current assignment toward the next retention. That retention may be with this client or another. If the consultant's personnel on this retention are already committed to another upcoming retention, the pressure is on the consultant to get the work done and to get on to the next project. This can on occasion adversely affect the final product.

DISPUTES

"A fundamental trend in the [management consulting] industry is the increased accountability of [management] consulting firms for their services. This trend is driven largely by client dissatisfaction with the level of service and analysis received as well as by clients publicly voicing their complaints. In 1997, a client of [a very large such firm] sued the firm on a charge that generic work was being peddled as unique analysis."[1]

Why Disputes Arise

One reason disputes arise is that the parties to the consulting relationship have entered into it for the wrong reasons:

- The consultant was retained when the project could have been, or should have been, adequately handled internally.
- The consultant was testing out new methodologies on the client.
- The consultant was retained to deliver a message that management already knew.
- Client personnel were not involved with the project, thus depriving the consultant of access to current information on the client.

Disputes also can arise because the parties have failed to handle the retention properly:

- The parties were operating under a poor definition of the project or the scope of work involved.
- The parties had no clear, common understanding as to what the project outcomes were to be.
- The parties did not share a common understanding of how the project was to be conducted.
- The consultant did not deliver on the desired outcomes, either in terms of quantity or quality. This can be due to the lack of agreement on the outcomes or the lack of any way to determine if the outcomes were achieved.
- The quote for the project was either excessive for what was delivered or was inadequate for the work actually conducted. In the first case, the client feels deceived; in the latter, the consultant either feels undercompensated or decided to reduce the resources it allocated to the project.
- One of the parties, or both, poorly managed the project.

The parties to a consulting agreement may intend never to have a dispute, and in fact may expect that their contract covers every possible question that could arise between them; *nevertheless, disputes are inevitable:*

"If the consulting firm reports good news, it receives further assignments. If it's bad news, the rubber band is released and the consulting firm is catapulted far, far away. While it is tempting to view this trend as client misbehavior stemming from an emotional reaction to bad news, the cause is a basic lack of communications stemming from both sides of the consulting relationship. [Competitive Intelligence] reports are commissioned not for purely intellectual reasons of exploring the business environment, but more often to support an idea or initiative of the manager who commissioned them. If the client's agenda is not clearly communicated, conflicts are inevitable."[2]

- The parties may disagree about their particular rights or obligations under the agreement, no matter how carefully the document was written and no matter how detailed were the specifications of the performance required by each side.
- These disputes may, in turn, lead to delays in performance and complaints about the quality of the consultant's work.
- Disputes may arise because of assertions that the client retaining the consultant has not cooperated with the consultant, making the consultant's work unnecessarily more difficult, or similar operational misunderstandings.

Unfortunately, even with the best of intentions, the parties to any agreement may end up delivering less than they initially promised in writing.

How to Deal with Disputes

When the parties to a consulting agreement face a dispute, the first question should be whether the consulting agreement covers the subject of the dispute. If the two parties have thought through their relationship thoroughly, their agreement likely has some provision governing the subject of the dispute. If so, the consultant and the client should be able to arrive at an amicable conclusion.

For example, if according to the consulting agreement the consultant's performance "must be satisfactory" to the client and the client's determination of whether the work or product is satisfactory must be made in good faith, the fact that the consulting agreement covers the subject may not resolve a dispute. The courts have held that the question of the existence of good faith requires an examination not only of the parties' own statements but also of how they actually behave. This means that a clause such as this one requires both good faith and a demonstration of good faith. For example, if a client asserts it cannot use a consultant's final report, *and* does not in fact use it, in a trial a court will probably find the client acted in good faith, even if the consultant can show that some other client could use it. But if the court finds that the client's officers were concerned about the high cost of the retention (even if the cost is as originally estimated) and then rejected the report, it will probably find the client acted in bad faith. Of course, good faith is in the eye of the beholder; a demonstration of good faith can still result in a breakdown in negotiations and ultimately in charges of breach of contract. Whether the damaged party is the client or the consultant, before seeking to use the legal remedies available—that is, suits for breach of contract, specific performance, rescission, restitution, enforcement or liquidated damages clauses— or resorting to arbitration, mediation, or alternative dispute resolution the damaged party must follow several key steps.

First, determine, from an objective basis, what it is that each party was to do and what each expected of the other:

- Any party that feels it has been damaged by the other party should reread the contract and any amendments made to it, as well as any instructions that were exchanged between the parties. A surprising number of disputes arise in the commercial world between parties who have not taken this first step to see whether the agreement they have signed covers the disputed points.

- If the agreement does not cover the dispute, then the parties should look to the practice that has grown up between them in their relationship. Why? Because the courts often will look to common commercial practice to determine the rights of the parties where the contract is silent. This practice is indicated, first, by the conduct between the parties to a contract, and second, by what is commonly accepted in similar commercial relationships.

This establishes the standards against which any possible breach of contract should be measured.

Second, if a party to an agreement believes a breach of contract has occurred, it should begin immediately to document that breach as well as any damages it is suffering. Such damages may include delays, difficulties in obtaining replacement services, defaults caused in related contracts, and other impacts on its own customers and suppliers. For example, a consulting agreement that is clearly tied to a particular project can result in various kinds of harm to either party. If the contract is breached by the client, the consultant may find that an alternative source of income has been cut off if the consultant did not enter into another engagement because it was bound exclusively for a time to the first. On the other hand, the client that believes it has suffered a breach of contract may find that the project for which it has hired the consultant is now in jeopardy. In either case, careful documentation should be the rule.

Third, communication between the parties in the case of a possible breach of contract should be conducted carefully. To the greatest extent possible, communication should be in writing to make sure there is a clear understanding between the parties regarding the grievance. The parties already should have made sure that their communications relating to the contract, particularly changes in performance and dates, were required to be in writing, and were in fact written in some form. Written communication not only protects the parties from violating the statute of frauds, as mentioned earlier, but protects their positions in the face of possible disputes over the contract. Although something in writing can be ambiguous, a written record is substantially easier to review than the incomplete recollection of the parties elicited after a falling out.

If the dispute cannot be resolved by negotiation, then the parties have two tracks they may pursue—litigation (a lawsuit) or nonlitigious means.

WHAT YOU CAN SUE FOR

When one party suffers a breach of contract, the only legal remedy most people think of is a lawsuit to collect money damages. In fact, the remedies available in court to the parties to a consulting contract are varied. Each remedy has its special benefits but also suffers from some limitations. The list includes:

- Damages for breach of contract, including liquidated damages;
- Restitution and equitable remedies;
- Specific performance;
- Rescission; and
- Suits to force the party to arbitration or mediation instead.

Damages

The legal principle underlying a suit for breach of contract says that if one party breaches an agreement, the other party may collect the damages necessary to put it in the

233

same position it would have been in had the contract been performed. What does that mean for the client and the consultant?

- If the consultant is to be paid a fixed fee, then clearly the fixed fee can be a measure of damages. If a contract is not completed and the consultant is to be paid on an hourly basis or on a percentage of money saved, then the damages may be too conjectural for a court to award.
- From the point of view of the client, it may be purchasing the expertise and services of a consultant to solve an unknown problem or to come up with new concepts, and it may have no idea of the value of the work if it was not all completed. This means that the client may not be able to sue for breach of contract, simply because it cannot show how it has been damaged.

So under contract law while the parties to a consulting agreement may have a right to sue, a party may not be able to prove the damages it actually suffered. And if a party cannot prove damages, a court will not generate them out of whole cloth.

Restitution and Equitable Remedies

Restitution is a way of collecting damages, but with a different legal tradition. The process here is to dissolve the contract, rather than enforce it, and by dissolving it, to restore parties to their original positions. In a restitution suit, the courts try to restore to each party the money it spent and then try to exchange additional money that compensates the parties for expenses they incurred.

Related to this are equitable remedies whereby the parties to a broken contract sue for value. For example, the consultant might sue the client to collect the value of his or her services to the client. An alternative is for the consultant to sue for the value of the services provided by it but measured in terms of lost time for the consultant who bills by the hour. For the client, the same choice of remedies exists—that is, to obtain a return of money spent or some return of value.

Because the consultant and the client may differ in their assessment of the value of the services rendered, the type of lawsuit that is brought can be critical. Therefore, there are rules about which remedy is available to whom and when. These rules seek to make sure that the courts reach the fairest and most equitable solution to a disputed agreement.

Rescission

Rescission of an agreement is an effort to eliminate the agreement and then return the parties to the status they would have occupied if the agreement had never existed. That is, the parties wash their hands of the whole affair and are put back to the position they occupied before they signed a contract. In some cases rescission may yield a result similar to that provided by restitution, particularly when the case involves the purchase and sale of goods.

In the case of contracts wherein services are exchanged for money, such as in consulting contracts, rescission is a difficult remedy to obtain from the courts. That is because there is no real physical commodity to transfer and return. For example, rescission can be obtained easily in the sale of a car. There, the court can force one party to return the car and the other to return the money. In the case of services, although one party can return the money, the services themselves cannot be returned. In fact, it is very hard, if not impossible, for a court to force a party completely to disgorge the benefits of services received, for once they have been rendered they, and their benefits, can never be returned.

Specific Performance

In the case of a services contract, such as the consulting agreement, a frequent remedy sought by an injured party is specific performance. There one party sues the other, asking the court to force the defending party to live up to the terms of the contract.

- If the client is successfully sued by the consultant, the client is forced to cooperate with the consultant in the performance of the consultant's services, to pay the consultant under the terms and conditions agreed upon, and generally to restore relations as if they had never broken down.
- If the client is suing the consultant, the court could order the consultant to perform the services promised in the contract under the same standards of care, good faith, and timeliness.

However, there is a class of service contracts, known as contracts for personal services, where these rules may not apply. The courts generally have held the following to be the way to define a personal services contract: The performance or work promised under the agreement is always personal and is never able to be delegated.

This category is based on the historical concept that the party seeking performance—here the client—entered into a contract with the consultant *only* on the condition that all the services are performed by an individual who, presumably, possesses unique skills. And the more unusual the skills, the more difficult it is for the court to secure performance.

In the past, courts refused to enforce personal services contracts because they had no way to ensure adequate compliance. The courts reasoned that any way a court has at its disposal to force a person to perform, including cash penalties and even the threat of prison, would take away the "spirit" of the performance.

The very oldest cases go back to the owners of theaters who wanted opera singers to honor their contract and appear. The courts said that the parties clearly had intended an opera singer to perform in a skillful, professional manner, but the courts were unable to enforce this agreement, as they had no way to judge the quality of the performance, and even if they had, they had no way acceptable in modern society to insist that the performance be done and be done properly. The courts themselves would not get involved in deciding whether the service was adequate.

Over time, the courts arrived at a compromise between the interests of the parties to such agreements, in our case the client and the consultant. When services are clearly personal and unique, the courts have continued to hold that they cannot force a person of high skills to perform under such a contract. However, the courts can in many cases keep such a skilled individual from entering into a contract to perform the same services for another person, usually a competitor.

The courts feel that if a skilled professional, here the consultant, wishes to refrain from performing special services, they cannot prevent him or her from doing so. But they can prevent him or her from breaching an agreement with the client by working for another person and performing the same services. The courts have noted slyly that if the effect of this order is to bring the two disputing parties together again, then they are all for it.

So when a contract with a consultant states that the services to be provided are to be the services of one or a few specifically designated individuals, the contract may be regarded as one for personal services. Therefore, given the limits on specific performance, the parties should be extremely careful when specifying that the client insists that the services being performed under the contract be those of one individual only.

It is clear today that the specific performance of a commercial agreement will not be prevented by the courts solely on the grounds that the performance requires the personal involvement of the defendant, but the courts are still reluctant to interfere and to supervise the day-to-day performance of highly skilled and talented individuals.

The following paragraph is one way of handling disputes. It is designed to deal with a situation in which the work done by the consultant may be in several different areas. So if there is a dispute, the parties would not know to which court they may take their case. A clause agreeing that a particular court has jurisdiction over the case will generally be respected by the courts if that jurisdiction has some reasonable relationship to the performance of the contract. The parties would fill in the name of the court and of the state, or even county, where indicated. The last part is included for cases where the parties have specified the U.S. District Courts, but where a U.S. District Court refuses to take the case. These courts will not accept a case between two persons it sees as residing in the same state. The court's concept of residing is substantially broader than the normal concept. For example, a corporation can be residing in the state where it is incorporated or where its principal place of business is. Therefore, this provides that the state courts have jurisdiction.

The _____ Court shall have jurisdiction with respect to all matters arising under this Agreement. The Consultant and the Client submit themselves to the jurisdiction of the _____ Court for all purposes; provided, however, if the said court shall lack jurisdiction, the [_____ State] Court shall have jurisdiction with respect to all matters hereunder and the parties hereby submit themselves to the jurisdiction of the [_____ State] Court for all purposes.

NONLITIGIOUS OPTIONS

Increasingly, businesses are seeking and using dispute resolution procedures that do not require lawsuits.

Mediation

Mediation is not generally regarded as a legal remedy in breach of contract. Mediation is rather the bringing in of another party to bridge the differences between the parties so that they can work out an amicable settlement.

- It is not the same as arbitration, as the recommendations of the mediator are not binding.
- It gives the parties a chance to review their cases and communicate their differences to a third party who has not participated in the transaction and who, it is hoped, can bring a more detached point of view.

If the parties use a mediator properly, they may find they can solve their problems simply by entering into a new or amended consulting agreement covering the problem that has arisen, settling the dispute it has engendered, and perhaps making some adjustments in compensation or performance, or both.

A mediator should be someone trusted by each party, but whom neither party feels is too closely aligned with the other. A potential source of mediators may be the professional organizations of which a consultant may be a member. Although many of these organizations cannot discipline their members formally, they do make available to their members, and in some cases to outsiders, a place where disputes can be aired. In fact, using these organizations as sources for mediators can be productive, as it permits each party to a dispute to make its case and air grievances without souring what may be an important commercial rela-

239

tionship by resorting to a more formal procedure, that is, a lawsuit or even arbitration.

Complaints to Organizations

Consultants tend to belong to voluntary organizations, both to learn more about their profession and to network—that is, to develop contacts leading to future retentions. Many of these organizations have some sort of code of ethics or professional standards that apply to their members. Some also advertise that they have ways of handling complaints against their members.

Before deciding to complain to an organization about the conduct of a consultant, the client should find out what its standards actually cover. Research shows that such standards cover a wide range of issues from professional behavior and confidentiality of client information to the proper use of the designation of membership in the association. Having found out what the standards cover, a client should next find out whether and to what extent the organization has a mechanism for enforcing the standards on its members. Experience shows that enforcement mechanisms for professional and ethical standards vary widely. Here is an example of what a client may find:

- One organization, containing people from virtually all management sciences, has no mechanism to ensure compliance with its standards of ethics.
- Other organizations require that all members must agree to abide by their code of ethics or forfeit membership, but they do not have any enforcement process.
- In some cases, there is an elaborate disciplinary procedure. These procedures can include a hearing and an investigation by the organization, and the ultimate discipline for a violation is suspension or expulsion.

Not all problems a client faces with a consultant will be of an ethical nature. The question, then, is whether voluntary membership organizations can handle complaints against their members that do not rise to the level of ethical problems. The general pattern is that most voluntary membership organizations do not have a procedure for handling complaints against their members apart from their professional or ethical standards. To the extent that they do, the receipt of complaints is handled formally; the complaints are reviewed to determine if they allege any violation of the ethical standards of the organization.

Of those few organizations that do, most fall into one of several models:

- The officers/directors of the organization try to settle complaints against members informally.
- The association receives complaints against members, and asks its members to explain the complaints, in a effort to encourage resolution, but it does not do more than that.
- The association offers arbitration to its members in disputes with nonmembers.

The majority of professional groups do not become involved in any way in such disputes. Some have taken this position because they are concerned about potentially violating the antitrust laws. From time to time, the U.S. Department of Justice has sought to bring the activities of professional and trade associations under the federal antitrust laws. The government position has been that such trade organizations often use codes of ethics and enforcement procedures, including expulsion, as a way of fixing prices or engaging in other anticompetitive practices. Given this concern, anything that the trade associations fear could have the effect of fixing prices or affecting competitive bidding is out of bounds. In practice, this means that the nonmember company often cannot hope to obtain any help from the organization if a member's conduct is alleged to have some element dealing with pricing practices, even if it is an ethical violation.

ASSISTANCE PROVIDED
IN YOUR CONSULTING AGREEMENT

In the agreement, the parties can handle anticipated disputes in two ways. They can insert a liquidated damages clause, one that provides a kind of penalty for specific breaches of contract, or they can provide that any unresolved disputes will go to arbitration or alternative dispute resolution to be resolved.

Liquidated Damages

One way to handle the performance of unique services by the consultant, or the provision of unique support services by the client, is to use a liquidated damage clause. This states that if a party breaches a contract, that party agrees to pay a set amount of damages to the other party.

The Client and the Consultant agree that any material violation of this Agreement will carry with it liquidated damages of $[amount].

These clauses originally were intended to meet the problem in the breach-of-contract cases discussed earlier, where the courts were unable to decide how much a party had been injured by the breach by another party to the contract.

Liquidated damage clauses often spawn more lawsuits than they prevent, however. After liquidated damage clauses were accepted, some parties to commercial agreements went to the extreme and inserted liquidated damage clauses of high amounts to prevent the party from breaching the contract with the threat of an onerous fine.

The courts then decided not to enforce what they regarded as "penalty" clauses and to enforce only true liquidated damage clauses. In general, this means that the courts will seek to determine whether, at the signing of the contract, the damages agreed upon were reasonably related to the foreseeable losses that could be incurred by the parties to the contract. They will reject enforcing damage clauses that are so high they constitute a penalty or direct threat to the livelihood of one of the parties to the contract.

In practice, this means that the parties must review the major potential breaches of contract in advance and assign a dollar value to them at the beginning of the contract. Not only is this extremely difficult, but it is an unusual subject to inject into the negotiations. Parties who have negotiated in good faith to arrive at a workable agreement then must sit down and decide the most likely ways either or both of them may break that contract *and* what value they should attach to each of those potential breaches.

The net result is that these clauses are few and far between. They are more common in commercial agreements where commodities or financial options are involved, that is, where the parties can see that money will be at stake and make an estimate in good faith of potential losses at the beginning of the contract. These good-faith estimates generally are upheld.

Arbitration and Alternative Dispute Resolution

Controversies arising out of most consulting agreements seldom involve major legal issues. They usually concern evaluation of facts and interpretation of one or two contract terms. When differences arise out of day-to-day commercial relations such as the consulting relationship, many parties prefer to settle them privately and informally in a businesslike manner that encourages continued relationships. That is why many businesses use commercial arbitration or alternative dispute resolution.

These options have been used increasingly for several reasons:

- First, crowded court calendars make it profitable to resolve disputes without resorting to the judicial process.
- Second, many groups have worked to educate businesspeople about the benefits and effectiveness of nonjudicial options.
- Third, it often makes sense to avoid the courts and obtain a quick decision by experts in the area in dispute.

Arbitration is a proceeding in which disputes are submitted for decision by a panel of individuals instead of by a judge. Generally, arbitration occurs in two situations:

- The parties to a contract agree in the contract to submit any future disputes to arbitration; or
- The parties involved in a current dispute agree to avoid a lawsuit and submit the dispute to arbitration.

The kinds of disputes that can go to arbitration are limited only by the terms of the arbitration agreement.

If the parties to a consulting agreement have inserted an arbitration clause, they will likely use the offices of the American Arbitration Association (AAA) to carry forward the arbitration, although this is not necessary. Some contract clauses specifically provide for arbitration by the AAA under its rules. If the parties wish to provide for this in advance, they should use the AAA arbitration clause shown here. The blank should be filled in with the city and state of the nearest regional office of the AAA. The last sentence ensures that either party seeking arbitration may begin the process without having to convince the other party to move to arbitration.

> Arbitration. Any controversy or claim arising out of, or relating to, this Agreement or the breach thereof shall be settled at _____ in accordance with the rules then obtaining of the American Arbitration Association. Judgment on the award may be entered in any court having jurisdiction thereof. This Agreement constitutes the voluntary submission of both parties to such arbitration.

While the term *alternative dispute resolution* (ADR) sometimes encompasses virtually every approach that avoids a civil court, most often it is applied to so-called "private courts." Here the parties agree to go through what is a private trial, usually before a retired judge. They may try all of the issues they face or limit, in advance, the private trial to a few very critical ones or only to very large ones. Because it contemplates a trial, this kind of process tends to be limited to the very largest, and longest-term, relationships.

Because of that, such clauses should be drafted to fit the unique circumstances of the relationship. As a general rule, ADR clauses should cover the following topics:

- A commitment by both parties to the concept of ADR.
- An agreement to provide the administrative support needed to ensure early intervention in cases where there are conflicts.
- A specific waiver of the right to go to court until and unless the agreed-upon ADR process fails.
- Powerful incentives to encourage use of ADR. Typically these involve a "use it or lose it" concept providing for the waiver of all claims not promptly submitted to ADR.

- An ADR plan crafted to reflect the parties, the circumstances, and the specific issues involved in the retention. This covers topics such as the timing for each stage of the ADR, what kinds of claims are made and how, and how information will be collected.

While the parties may agree to be bound by the results of an ADR process, sometimes they do not. In those cases where they agree to be bound, the private trial ends the dispute. Even in cases where they did not agree to be bound, often the fact that a judge has found against them is enough to encourage a truculent client or consultant to settle the dispute without going further.

Parties also may provide by special agreement that, as long as the parties have fulfilled its terms, the results of an ADR, including any award, will be kept confidential. Unless the parties provide otherwise, these proceedings are held in private and are not a matter of public record. Thus, there is an additional level of flexibility, particularly when the parties may be disclosing sensitive commercial or business information they do not wish to be made public.

NOTES

1. Biswas and Twichell, *Management Consulting*, 24.
2. Garland, "CI Consultants and Clients," 31.

Appendix A

GLOSSARY

ADR Alternative dispute resolution.

Agency The relationship of one person acting for, or representing, another, by the authority of the other person. The other person is called the principal.

Alternative dispute resolution A wide variety of processes that allow businesses to handle legal disputes without going to civil court.

Arbitration Resolving a conflict or dispute by using a third party, selected by the two parties to the dispute.

Associate In general, any person associated with an enterprise. In business, the term was previously used to describe a person working with clients for a partnership who is not yet a partner. Now its use has been expanded by some enterprises to cover all employees.

Audit An independent, structured, and documented evaluation of the adequacy and implementation of an activity to specified requirements. It may examine any element of management control, such as financial, environmental, and quality aspects.

Beta test A term taken from software development, indicating the time during which a project is tested by outsiders rather than by its developers and designers. The term is now used to indicate a process or solution that works but is still subject to testing before it is refined.

Breach of contract A violation of or a failure to perform any or all parts of a contract without a valid legal excuse.

CEO Chief executive officer.

CFO Chief financial officer.

CIO Chief information officer.

Client A customer of a person or company that provides professional services. The term is now used to describe the customer of any service provider.

Consultant One who provides consulting services; an independent contractor.

Consulting Technically, the providing of advice by one person or entity to another. Over time, it has grown to deal with professional and/or technical advice. In current usage, it involves services as well as strictly advice.

Contract An enforceable agreement between two or more parties to do, or not to do, a particular thing. It can be written, oral, or implied.

COO Chief operating officer.

Customer A person or organization, internal or external, that receives or uses outputs from one group or division. Such outputs may be products, services, or information.

Damages An indemnity or a reparation in money that may be recovered by a person who has suffered an injury to his or her person, property, or rights because of the unlawful act, default, or negligence of another person.

Director   Someone who supervises a large number of people. In consulting firms, it is often used as an intermediate title between manager and partner or shareholder.

End users   Persons or organizations that request and use products or services provided by a contractor or consultant. End users are typically not the same as the person or unit that signs a contract for the products or services.

Engagement   Another term for a consulting assignment. See retention.

Independent contractor   A person who contracts to do certain work, according to his or her own methods, without control by the hiring party, except as to the result or product of that work.

Manager   Someone who supervises another. In consulting firms, it is often used as an intermediate title between associate and partner or shareholder.

Oral agreement   An agreement that is not written down but only expressed in the words used by the parties. Many oral agreements are made unenforceable by the statute of frauds.

Outsourcing   The process of arranging for entire business functions or processes to be handled by another company, governed by a long-term contract; contracting out business functions or processes to a third party. While the process may be transparent to third parties, such as customers, the firm providing the outsourced services or products typically retains control over the means and manner of performance; its obligation to its client is to provide the goods or services or specified quality against agreed-upon performance measures.

Partner One of several joint owners in a partnership. Partners share in both the profits and losses of the enterprise and are individually liable for its debts and losses.

P O Purchase order.

Practitioner One engaged in a particular practice, that is, business. The term is often used to describe an individual consultant.

Purchase order Document issued permitting the party receiving it to ship goods or provide services to the issuer. It ensures that terms covering the acquisition of the goods and services are under terms set by the purchaser and effectively guarantees payment as long as the terms of the purchase order are met.

Retention A consulting assignment. See engagement.

Request for Proposal A written document asking potential contractors to provide a statement of how they will carry out a potential project as well as how it is to be priced. It usually includes all the terms of any contract to be entered into by the person issuing it. If the proposal is accepted, the RFP constitutes a binding contract.

Request for Quotation A written document asking potential contractors to provide a statement of how much a specific project will cost to complete. It usually includes all the terms of any contract to be entered into by the person issuing it. If the price quoted is accepted, the RFQ constitutes a binding contract.

RFP Request for Proposal.

RFQ Request for Quotation.

SBU Strategic business unit.

Services contract A contract where one or more parties to the agreement provide services, rather than goods, to the other.

Shareholder One of the owners of an incorporated business. Shareholders share in the profits of an enterprise through dividends. Their liability for the debts and losses of the business is usually limited to the value of the shares they have purchased.

Strategic business unit   A portion of an enterprise, managed separately, usually encompassing a major portion of the parent company's activities. An SBU is so named for the fact that it tends to have to develop its own strategy.

Tort   Any legal wrong or harm.

Verbal agreement   A term erroneously used instead of oral agreement. Technically, a verbal agreement is one that is made in words. While there can be nonverbal agreements, the circumstances under which that can happen are severely limited.

Vicarious liability   The concept that attributes liability for acts of any employee in the course of employment to the employer.

Appendix B

EXTRACTS FROM SECTIONS 1 AND 2, IRS PUBLICATION NUMBER 15A, *EMPLOYER'S SUPPLEMENTAL TAX GUIDE (1999)*

1. WHO ARE EMPLOYEES?

Before you can know how to treat payments you make for services, you must first know the business relationship that exists between you and the person performing the services. The person performing the services may be—

- An independent contractor.
- A common-law employee.

- A statutory employee.
- A statutory nonemployee.

This discussion explains these four categories. A later discussion, **Employee or Independent Contractor?** (section 2), points out the differences between an independent contractor and an employee and gives examples from various types of occupations. If an individual who works for you is not an employee under the common-law rules (see section 2), you generally do not have to withhold Federal income tax from that individual's pay. However, in some cases you may be required to backup withhold on these payments. See Circular E for information on backup withholding.

Independent Contractors

People such as lawyers, contractors, subcontractors, public stenographers, and auctioneers who follow an independent trade, business, or profession in which they offer their services to the public, are generally not employees. However, whether such people are employees or independent contractors depends on the facts in each case. The general rule is that an individual is an independent contractor if you, the payer, have the right to control or direct only the result of the work and not the means and methods of accomplishing the result.

Common-Law Employees

Under common-law rules, anyone who performs services for you is your employee if you can control what will be done and how it will be done. This is so even when you give the employee freedom of action. What matters is that you have the right to control the details of how the services are performed. For a discussion of facts that indicate whether an individual providing services is an independent contractor or employee, see **Employee or Independent Contractor?** (section 2).

If you have an employer-employee relationship, it makes no difference how it is labeled. The **substance** of the relationship, **not the label,** governs the worker's status. Nor does it matter whether the individual is employed full time or part time.

For employment tax purposes, no distinction is made between classes of employees. Superintendents, managers, and other supervisory personnel are all employees. An **officer of a corporation** is generally an employee, but a **director** is not. An officer who performs no services or only minor services, and neither receives nor is entitled to receive any pay, is not considered an employee.

You generally have to withhold and pay income, social security, and Medicare taxes on wages you pay to common-law employees. However, the wages of certain employees may be exempt from one or more of these taxes. See **Employees of Exempt Organizations** (section 3) and **Religious Exemptions** (section 4).

Leased employees. Under certain circumstances, a corporation furnishing workers to various professional people and firms is the employer of those workers for employment tax purposes. For example, a professional service corporation may provide the services of secretaries, nurses, and other similarly trained workers to its subscribers.

The service corporation enters into contracts with the subscribers under which the subscribers specify the services to be provided and the fee to be paid to the service corporation for each individual furnished. The service corporation has the right to control and direct the worker's services for the subscriber, including the right to discharge or reassign the worker. The service corporation hires the workers, controls the payment of their wages, provides them with unemployment insurance and other benefits, and is the employer for employment tax purposes. For information on employee leasing as it relates to pension plan qualification requirements, see **Leased employees** in **Pub. 560,**

Retirement Plans for Small Business (SEP, SIMPLE, and Keogh Plans).

Additional information. For more information about the treatment of special types of employment, the treatment of special types of payments, and similar subjects, get Circular E or Circular A (for agricultural employers).

Statutory Employees

Four categories of workers who are independent contractors under common law are treated by statute as employees.

- A driver who distributes beverages (other than milk) or meat, vegetable, fruit, or bakery products; or who picks up and delivers laundry or dry cleaning, if the driver is your agent or is paid on commission.

- A full-time life insurance sales agent whose principal business activity is selling life insurance or annuity contracts, or both, primarily for one life insurance company.

- An individual who works at home on materials or goods that you supply and that must be returned to you or to a person you name, if you also furnish specifications for the work to be done.

- A full-time traveling or city salesperson who works on your behalf and turns in orders to you from wholesalers, retailers, contractors, or operators of hotels, restaurants, or other similar establishments. The goods sold must be merchandise for resale or supplies for use in the buyer's business operation. The work performed for you must be the salesperson's principal business activity. See **Salesperson** in section 2.

Social security and Medicare taxes. Withhold social security and Medicare taxes from statutory employees' wages if all three of the following conditions apply.

256

- The service contract states or implies that substantially all the services are to be performed personally by them.
- They do not have a substantial investment in the equipment and property used to perform the services (other than an investment in transportation facilities).
- The services are performed on a continuing basis for the same payer.

Federal unemployment (FUTA) tax. For FUTA tax, the term *employee* means the same as it does for social security and Medicare taxes, except that it does not include statutory employees in categories 2 and 3 above. Thus, any individual who is an employee under category 1 or 4 is also an employee for FUTA tax purposes and subject to FUTA tax.

Income tax. Do not withhold income tax from the wages of statutory employees.

Reporting payments to statutory employees. Furnish a Form W-2 to a statutory employee, and check "statutory employee" in box 15. Show your payments to the employee as other compensation in box 1. Also, show social security wages in box 3, social security tax withheld in box 4, Medicare wages in box 5, and Medicare tax withheld in box 6. The statutory employee can deduct his or her trade or business expenses from the payments shown on Form W-2. He or she reports earnings as a statutory employee on line 1 of Schedule C or C-EZ (Form 1040). (A statutory employee's business expenses are deductible on Schedule C or C-EZ (Form 1040) and are not subject to the reduction by 2% of his or her adjusted gross income that applies to common-law employees.)

Statutory Nonemployees

There are two categories of statutory nonemployees: *direct sellers* and *licensed real estate agents.* They are treated as self-employed for all Federal tax purposes, including income and employment taxes, if:

Substantially all payments for their services as direct sellers or real estate agents are directly related to sales or other output, rather than to the number of hours worked, and

Their services are performed under a written contract providing that they will not be treated as employees for Federal tax purposes.

Direct sellers. Direct sellers include persons falling within any of the following three groups:

Persons engaged in selling (or soliciting the sale of) consumer products in the home or place of business other than in a permanent retail establishment.

Persons engaged in selling (or soliciting the sale of) consumer products to any buyer on a buy-sell basis, a deposit-commission basis, or any similar basis prescribed by regulations, for resale in the home or at a place of business other than in a permanent retail establishment.

Persons engaged in the trade or business of delivering or distributing newspapers or shopping news (including any services directly related to such delivery or distribution).

Direct selling includes activities of individuals who attempt to increase direct sales activities of their direct sellers and who earn income based on the productivity of their direct sellers. Such activities include providing motivation and encouragement; imparting skills, knowledge, or experience; and recruiting. For more information on direct sellers, see **Pub. 911,** Direct Sellers.

Licensed real estate agents. This category includes individuals engaged in appraisal activities for real estate sales if they earn income based on sales or other output.

Misclassification of Employees

Consequences of treating an employee as an independent contractor. If you classify an employee as an independent contractor and you have no reasonable basis for doing so, you may be held liable for employment taxes for that worker (the relief provisions, discussed below, will not apply). See Internal Revenue Code section 3509 for more information.

Relief provisions. If you have a reasonable basis for not treating a worker as an employee, you may be relieved from having to pay employment taxes for that worker. To get this relief, you must file all required Federal information returns on a basis consistent with your treatment of the worker. You (or your predecessor) must not have treated any worker holding a substantially similar position as an employee for any periods beginning after 1977.

Technical service specialists. This relief provision does not apply to a worker who provides services to another business (the client) as a technical service specialist under an arrangement between the business providing the worker, such as a technical services firm, and the client. A technical service specialist is an engineer, designer, drafter, computer programmer, systems analyst, or other similarly skilled worker engaged in a similar line of work.

This rule does not affect the determination of whether such workers are employees under the common-law rules. The common-law rules control whether the specialist is treated as an employee or an independent contractor. However, if you directly contract with a technical service specialist to provide services for your business rather than for another business, you may still be entitled to the relief provision. See **Employee or Independent Contractor?** below.

2. EMPLOYEE OR INDEPENDENT CONTRACTOR?

An employer must generally withhold income taxes, withhold and pay social security and Medicare taxes, and pay unemployment tax on wages paid to an employee. An employer does not generally have to withhold or pay any taxes on payments to independent contractors.

Common-Law Rules

To determine whether an individual is an employee or an independent contractor under the common law, the relationship of the worker and the business must be examined. All evidence of control and independence must be considered. In any employee-independent contractor determination, all information that provides evidence of the degree of control and the degree of independence must be considered.

Facts that provide evidence of the degree of control and independence fall into three categories: behavioral control, financial control, and the type of relationship of the parties as shown below.

Behavioral control. Facts that show whether the business has a right to direct and control how the worker does the task for which the worker is hired include the type and degree of—

Instructions the business gives the worker. An employee is generally subject to the business' instructions about when, where, and how to work. All of the following are examples of types of instructions about how to do work:

- When and where to do the work.
- What tools or equipment to use.

260

- What workers to hire or to assist with the work.
- Where to purchase supplies and services.
- What work must be performed by a specified individual.
- What order or sequence to follow.

The amount of instruction needed varies among different jobs. Even if no instructions are given, sufficient behavioral control may exist if the employer has the right to control how the work results are achieved. A business may lack the knowledge to instruct some highly specialized professionals; in other cases, the task may require little or no instruction. The key consideration is whether the business has retained the right to control the details of a worker's performance or instead has given up that right.

Training the business gives the worker. An employee may be trained to perform services in a particular manner. Independent contractors ordinarily use their own methods.

Financial control. Facts that show whether the business has a right to control the business aspects of the worker's job include:

The extent to which the worker has unreimbursed business expenses. Independent contractors are more likely to have unreimbursed expenses than are employees. Fixed ongoing costs that are incurred regardless of whether work is currently being performed are especially important. However, employees may also incur unreimbursed expenses in connection with the services they perform for their business.

The extent of the worker's investment. An independent contractor often has a significant investment in the facilities he or she uses in performing services for someone else. However, a significant investment is not necessary for independent contractor status.

The extent to which the worker makes services available to the relevant market. An independent contractor is generally free to seek out business opportunities.

Independent contractors often advertise, maintain a visible business location, and are available to work in the relevant market.

How the business pays the worker. An employee is generally guaranteed a regular wage amount for an hourly, weekly, or other period of time. This usually indicates that a worker is an employee, even when the wage or salary is supplemented by a commission. An independent contractor is usually paid by a flat fee for the job. However, it is common in some professions, such as law, to pay independent contractors hourly.

The extent to which the worker can realize a profit or loss. An independent contractor can make a profit or loss.

Type of relationship. Facts that show the parties' type of relationship include:

- ***Written contracts describing the relationship the parties intended to create.***
- ***Whether the business provides the worker with employee-type benefits, such as insurance, a pension plan, vacation pay, or sick pay.***
- ***The permanency of the relationship.*** If you engage a worker with the expectation that the relationship will continue indefinitely, rather than for a specific project of period, this is generally considered evidence that your intent was to create an employer-employee relationship.
- ***The extent to which services performed by the worker are a key aspect of the regular business of the company.*** If a worker provides services that are a key aspect of your regular business activity, it is more likely that you will have the right to direct and control his or her activities. For example, if a law firm hires an attorney, it is likely that it will present the attorney's work as its own and would have the right to control or direct that work. This would indicate an employer-employee relationship.

- ***The extent to which services performed by the worker are a key aspect of the regular business of the company.*** If a worker provides services that are a key aspect of your regular business activity, it is more likely that you will have the right to direct and control his or her activities. For example, if a law firm hires an attorney, it is likely that it will present the attorney's work as its own and would have the right to control or direct that work. This would indicate an employer-employee relationship.

IRS help. If you want the IRS to determine whether a worker is an employee, file **Form SS-8.** Determination of Employee Work Status for Purposes of Federal Employment Taxes and Income Tax Withholding, with the IRS.

Industry Examples

The following examples may help you properly classify your workers.

Building and Construction Industry
Example 1. Jerry Jones has an agreement with Wilma White to supervise the remodeling of her house. She did not advance funds to help him carry on the work. She makes direct payments to the suppliers for all necessary materials. She carries liability and workers' compensation insurance covering Jerry and others he engaged to assist him. She pays them an hourly rate and exercises almost constant supervision over the work. Jerry is not free to transfer his assistants to other jobs. He may not work on other jobs while working for Wilma. He assumes no responsibility to complete the work and will incur no contractual liability if he fails to do so. He and his assistants perform personal services for hourly wages. They are employees of Wilma White.

Example 2. Milton Manning, an experienced tilesetter, orally agreed with a corporation to perform full-time services at construction sites. He uses his own tools and performs services in the order designated by the corporation and according to its specifications. The corporation supplies all materials, makes frequent inspections of his work, pays him on a piecework basis, and carries workers' compensation insurance on him. He does not have a place of business or hold himself out to perform similar services for others. Either party can end the services at any time. Milton Manning is an employee of the corporation.

Example 3. Wallace Black agreed with the Sawdust Co. to supply the construction labor for a group of houses. The company agreed to pay all construction costs. However, he supplies all the tools and equipment. He performs personal services as a carpenter and mechanic for an hourly wage. He also acts as superintendent and foreman and engages other individuals to assist him. The company has the right to select, approve, or discharge any helper. A company representative makes frequent inspections of the construction site. When a house is finished, Wallace is paid a certain percentage of its costs. He is not responsible for faults, defects of construction, or wasteful operation. At the end of each week, he presents the company with a statement of the amount he has spent, including the payroll. The company gives him a check for that amount from which he pays the assistants, although he is not personally liable for their wages. Wallace Black and his assistants are employees of the Sawdust Co.

Example 4. Bill Plum contracted with Elm Corporation to complete the roofing on a housing complex. A signed contract established a flat amount for the services rendered by Bill Plum. Bill is a licensed roofer and carries workers' compensation and liability insurance under the business name, Plum Roofing. He hires his own roofers who are treated as employees for Federal employment tax purposes. If there is a problem with the roofing work, Plum Roofing is responsible for paying for any repairs. Bill Plum, doing business as Plum Roofing, is an independent contractor.

Example 5. Vera Elm, an electrician, submitted a job estimate to a housing complex for electrical work at $16 per hour for 400 hours. She is to receive $1,280 every 2 weeks for the next 10 weeks. This is not considered payment by the hour. Even if she works more or less than 400 hours to complete the work, Vera Elm will receive $6,400. She also performs additional electrical installations under contracts with other companies, which she obtained through advertisements. Vera is an independent contractor.

Trucking Industry

Example. Rose Trucking contracts to deliver material for Forest Inc. at $140 per ton. Rose Trucking is not paid for any articles that are not delivered. At times, Jan Rose, who operates as Rose Trucking, may also lease another truck and engage a driver to complete the contract. All operating expenses, including insurance coverage, are paid by Jan Rose. All equipment is owned or rented by Jan, and she is responsible for all maintenance. None of the drivers are provided by Forest Inc. Jan Rose, operating as Rose Trucking, is an independent contractor.

Computer Industry

Example. Steve Smith, a computer programmer, is laid off when Megabyte Inc. downsizes Megabyte agrees to pay Steve a flat amount to complete a one-time project to create a certain product. It is not clear how long it will take to complete the project, and Steve is not guaranteed any minimum payment for the hours spent on the program. Megabyte provides Steve with no instructions beyond the specifications for the product itself. Steve and Megabyte have a written contract, which provides that Steve is considered to be an independent contractor, is required to pay Federal and state taxes, and receives no benefits from Megabyte. Megabyte will file a Form 1099-MISC. Steve does the work on a new high-end computer which cost him

$7,000. Steve works at home and is not expected or allowed to attend meetings of the software development group. Steve is an independent contractor.

Automobile Industry

Example 1. Donna Lee is a salesperson employed on a full-time basis by Bob Blue, an auto dealer. She works 6 days a week and is on duty in Bob's showroom on certain assigned days and times. She appraises trade-ins, but her appraisals are subject to the sales manager's approval. Lists of prospective customers belong to the dealer. She has to develop leads and report results to the sales manager. Because of her experience, she requires only minimal assistance in closing and financing sales and in other phases of her work. She is paid a commission and is eligible for prizes and bonuses offered by Bob. Bob also pays the cost of health insurance and group-term life insurance for Donna. Donna is an employee of Bob Blue.

Example 2. Sam Sparks performs auto repair services in the repair department of an auto sales company. He works regular hours and is paid on a percentage basis. He has no investment in the repair department. The sales company supplies all facilities, repair parts, and supplies, issues instructions on the amounts to be charged, parts to be used, and the time for completion of each job, and checks all estimates and repair orders. Sam is an employee of the sales company.

Example 3. An auto sales agency furnishes space for Helen Bach to perform auto repair services. She provides her own tools, equipment, and supplies. She seeks out business from insurance adjusters and other individuals and does all the body and paint work that comes to the agency. She hires and discharges her own helpers, determines her own and her helpers' working hours, quotes prices for repair work, makes all necessary adjustments, assumes all losses from uncollectible accounts, and receives, as compensation for her services, a large percentage of the gross collections from the auto repair shop.

Helen is an independent contractor and the helpers are her employees.

Attorney

Example. Donna Yuma is a sole practitioner who rents office space and pays for the following items: telephone, computer, on-line legal research linkup, fax machine, and photocopier. Donna buys office supplies and pays bar dues and membership dues for three other professional organizations. Donna has a part-time receptionist who also does the bookkeeping. She pays the receptionist, withholds and pays Federal and state employment taxes, and files a Form W-2 each year. For the past 2 years, Donna has had only three clients, corporations with which there have been long-standing relationships. Donna charges the corporations an hourly rate for her services, sending monthly bills detailing the work performed for the prior month. The bills include charges for long distance calls, on-line research time, fax charges, photocopies, postage, and travel, costs for which the corporations have agreed to reimburse her. Donna is an independent contractor.

Taxicab Driver

Example. Tom Spruce rents a cab from Taft Cab Co. for $150 per day. He pays the costs of maintaining and operating the cab. Tom Spruce keeps all fares he receives from customers. Although he receives the benefit of Taft's two-way radio communication equipment, dispatcher, and advertising, these items benefit both Taft and Tom Spruce. Tom Spruce is an independent contractor.

Salesperson

To determine whether salespersons are employees under the usual common-law rules, you must evaluate each individual case. If a salesperson who works for you does not meet the tests for a common-law employee, discussed earlier, you do not have to withhold income tax from his or her pay (see **Statutory Employees** earlier). However, even if a salesperson is not an employee under the usual common-law rules, his or her pay may still be subject to social security, Medicare, and FUTA taxes. To determine whether a salesperson is an employee for social security, Medicare, and FUTA tax purposes, the salesperson must meet **all** eight elements of the statutory employee test. A salesperson is an employee for social security, Medicare, and FUTA tax purposes if he or she:

Works full time for one person or company except, possibly, for sideline sales activities on behalf of some other person,

Sells on behalf of, and turns his or her orders over to, the person or company for which he or she works,

Sells to wholesalers, retailers, contractors, or operators of hotels, restaurants, or similar establishments,

Sells merchandise for resale, or supplies for use in the customer's business,

Agrees to do substantially all of this work personally,

Has no substantial investment in the facilities used to do the work, other than in facilities for transportation,

Maintains a continuing relationship with the person or company for which he or she works, and

Is not an employee under common-law rules.

INDEX

Index